Bernadette la Porte 6./91.

SHIN NIHONGO NO KISO I

MAIN TEXTBOOK
ROMANIZED EDITION

しんにほんごのきそ I

SHIN NIHONGO NO KISO I

MAIN TEXTBOOK
ROMANIZED EDITION

しんにほんごのきそⅠ

THE ASSOCIATION FOR OVERSEAS TECHNICAL SCHOLARSHIP (AOTS)

3A Corporation

Shoei Bldg. 6F, 6-3, Sarugaku-cho 2-chome, Chiyoda-ku, Tokyo, 101 Japan

© 3A Corporation 1990

First published in Japan by 3A Corporation 1990

ISBN4-906224-50-4 C0081
Printed in Japan

序

　財団法人海外技術者研修協会は、1959年に設立されて以来、アジア・アフリカ・ラテンアメリカの発展途上諸国の技術研修生の受入れ及び研修に関する事業を行ってきた。1989年3月末現在、受入れ研修生数は延べ約4万人、受入れ対象国は150ヶ国に及んでいる。

　研修生が、日本で生活し企業で研修を受ける際、研修生にとって最大の悩みは言葉である。日本語が分からなければ、日本になじめないし、日本を知ることも難しく、工場実習の成果を十分には期待できない。研修の成果と日本語習得の度合いとは、多くの場合、比例関係にあるということが私たち協会の経験的結論である。この意味で、協会は創立以来、在日期間の比較的短い技術研修生に対しての日本語教育を重視してきた。

　協会の日本語教育は、企業の実地研修に先立って行われる一般研修の一環として行われている。現在、日本語を主要科目とする一般研修には、6週間コース（日本語100時間）と13週間コース（日本語200時間）とがある。中心は、6週間コースで、時間にして100時間弱である。言葉の教育として異例に短いが、これは、研修生の滞在期間が限られていて、且つ、来日の目的が技術習得であることに鑑み、できるだけ多くの時間を実地研修に充当しなければならないからである。このため、私たちは、最も効率的な、短時間に具体的成果のあがる方法を、常に工夫してきた。これが私たち協会で教える日本語である。

　そこで、1961年協会独自の教科書『Practical Japanese Conversation』が作られ、1964年改訂版、1965年再訂版が作成された。この二度にわたる改訂によるも、なお、「覚えやすい」「すぐに役立つ」「一定の品位を保つ」協会の日本語の教科書としては，十分に満足できるまでに至らなかった。

　そのため、1967年には、新たな構想のもとに『実用日本語会話』（Practical Japanese Conversation）を作成した。そして2年後にはその各国語版（5ヶ国語）も完成した。しかしながら、実際に用いてみると、この『実用日本語会話』は100時間短期集中教育の教科書としては盛り沢山であることが分かった。したがって、更に研究と検討を重ねて編纂されたものが、『日本語の基礎』（後の『日本語の基礎Ⅰ』）である。その後、日本語学習歴のある研修生の増加及び一般研修13週間コースの常設化に対応して、『日本語の基礎Ⅱ』を1981年に刊行した。

『日本語の基礎Ⅰ』は、よく長年の風雪に耐えてきた。今後も長く耐え続けるかも知れないと思われた。しかし、何分にも、刊行後すでに10年以上の歳月を経ている。また、この間研修生の大幅な増加と、研修生の国や日本語学習歴の多様化が一層進んでいた。そこで新たな時代の要求に応えるため、またⅠとⅡとを統一的に見直す必要から、1985年に改訂に着手し、検討と試用を積み重ねて、この度『新日本語の基礎Ⅰ』の完成を見るに至った。

　この教科書は、研修協会が対象とする技術研修生の100時間コース用として編纂されたものではあるが、教科書の説明を読み、その指示に従うならば、一般の短期学習者、あるいは入門期の日本語教育にも十分活用できるものと確信している。

　この改訂にあたっては、各方面からの御助言を得た。深く感謝申し上げると共に、本書の活用と協会の日本語教育の充実のため、更に一層の御支援をお願いする次第である。

1989年11月

財団法人　海外技術者研修協会

専務理事　山本長昭

改訂にあたって

　『日本語の基礎Ⅰ』と『日本語の基礎Ⅱ』はその作成時期において、10年近く
の開きがある。そのためⅠからⅡを通してみると、内容的に統一を欠く面が残っ
た。このような内容の是正と共に、これまでの教授法の反省を踏まえて、1985年
より、『日本語の基礎Ⅰ・Ⅱ』の全面的改訂に踏み切った。改訂にあたり、留意し
た点は以下の通りである。

　1．まず、基本的で使用頻度の高い日本語の文型、語彙、表現などを再検討し、
　　　内容の刷新を図った。更に、文型、例文、会話、練習など、教科書全体の構
　　　成を立て直した。

　2．『日本語の基礎』の文型練習の積み上げによる文型、語彙の定着の良さとい
　　　う長所を生かしながらも、会話の実際的な運用力が向上するように「練習Ｃ」
　　　を加えた。

　3．研修生及び、技術研修先の会社や工場の方々の協力を仰いで、研修生が来
　　　日してから帰国するまでの言語活動を調査した。この中から、研修生が日本
　　　語を使用する場面、状況などを選び、「会話」に反映させた。「会話」は簡潔
　　　な表現で、しかも実用性が高く、自然な日本語であることに留意した。

　4．数課ごとの復習、文法事項のまとめ、関連語彙などを加え、学習者、教授
　　　者にも教科書として使いやすくなるように配慮した。

　5．日本語学習の初期段階における聞き取り力の養成を重視し、「問題」に聞き
　　　取りの内容を多く取り入れた。また、読解力を養う導入として、短い内容の
　　　読み物を配した。

　『新日本語の基礎Ⅰ』は、上記の意図に基づく初級レベルの日本語教科書であ
る。学習時間は約100時間である。2年間の試用期間を置き、検討、補正を重ね、
発刊に至った。しかし、まだなお不十分な点があると思われる。多くの方々の御
批判、御助言をいただき、より一層の充実を目指したい。

凡　例

I．教科書の構成

　この教科書は本冊、分冊、及びカセットテープより成る。本冊はローマ字版と漢字か
なまじり版の2種類がある。分冊は英語、インドネシア語、タイ語、スペイン語、韓国
語、中国語がある。他の言語についても、順次完成させていく予定である。

　この教科書は日本語を聞く、話すということを中心に構成されている。従って、ひら
がな、かたかな、漢字などの文字の読み書きの指導は含んでいない。

II．教科書の内容及び使い方

1．本冊

1）日本語の発音

　日本語の発音上注意すべき点について、主な例を提出してある。この上になお、学
習者の個々の母国語の背景を考慮した練習をすることが望ましい。

2）教室の言葉、挨拶、数字

　教師の指示、日常の基本的挨拶などで、本課に入ってからもよく使われるものなの
で、しっかり練習しておく。

3）本課

　1課から25課まであり、内容は以下のように分けられる。

① 文型

　その課で学ぶ基本文型を提出順序に従って掲げてある。

② 例文

　基本文型を質問及び答えという対話の形式で表してある。文型が実際にどのよう
に用いられているかを談話の最小単位の形で示したものである。また、その課で扱
われた副詞や接続詞などの使い方をできるだけ取り上げた。基本文型に示された以
外のその課で学ぶ学習項目も入っている。

③ 会話

　会話の登場人物はセンターで6週間の一般研修を受ける研修生達を中心として、
コース開始から研修先へ赴くまでの話しをまとめてある。各課の学習内容を密着さ
せた形で日常生活によく使用される挨拶などの慣用的表現を加えて作成した。平易
な会話であるから、全文暗記することが望ましい。余裕があれば、分冊の関連語彙
表や視聴覚教材などを利用して、この会話を発展させ、会話力の向上に役立たせて
ほしい。

④ 練習

　練習はA，B，Cの三段階に分かれる。練習Aは文法的な構造を理解しやすいよ
うに、視覚的効果を考えてレイアウトしてある。基本的な文型を語彙の代入という
形で定着を図ると共に、活用形の作り方、後続句への品詞別の接続の仕方などを学
びやすく配慮してある。

　練習Bは様々なドリル形式を用いて、基本文型の定着の強化を図るものである。
☞ の印のついた番号は絵チャートを用いる練習を示す。

　練習Cは練習A，Bの基礎的な文型練習が円滑に出来るようになった段階で行う

短い会話練習ドリルである。文型が実際にどのような場面、状況の中で、その機能を果たすかを学ばせ、発話力を高めるために設けた。教科書のまま読み上げたり、単にリピートするだけではなく、クラスのレベルや状況に合わせて、モデル文の代入肢を変えたり、さらに練習の展開を図るような工夫が望まれる。

⑤ 問題

　問題には，聞き取り（ 🔲 マークの箇所）と文法問題とがある。聞き取りはカセットテープを聞いて、短い質問に答える問題と、短い会話のやりとりを聞いて内容の要点を把握する問題とがある。これらの問題は聞き取りの力の強化を図るために設けた。文法問題は、語彙やその課で学んだ文法事項の理解度を確認するものである。読解問題は既習語彙、文型を使って書き下した平易な文を読んで、その内容に関する質問に答えるものが多い。

⑥ 復習

　数課ごとに学習事項の要点を再整理するために設けた。

⑦ まとめ

　本冊の終わりに、この教科書に提出された助詞や動詞のいろいろなフォームの使い方、副詞や接続詞などの文法事項を項目ごとにまとめ、例文を掲げた。

⑧ 索引

　本冊の教室の言葉、挨拶、数字をはじめ、各課の新出語彙、表現などが載せてある。

2．分冊

分冊はPARTⅠからPARTⅣまでの４つの内容に分かれる。

① PARTⅠ　語彙及び訳

　各課の新出語彙とその各国語訳が載せてある。これらは絵教材化されて市販されている。

② PARTⅡ　関連語彙及び訳

　必須語彙ではないが、役に立つと思われる語彙を中心に、13項目に分けてまとめた。

③ PARTⅢ　翻訳

　本冊中の発音編、教室の言葉、挨拶、文型、例文、会話及びまとめの部分の各国語訳である。

④ PARTⅣ　付表

　数字、時の表現、期間の表し方、助数詞など、この教科書で提出されている語彙面の学習内容を整理し、更に多少項目を追加した。

3．表記上の注意

１）表記は原則として、ヘボン式による。

　　撥音はすべて "n" で表記した。

２）長母音は以下のように表記した。

　　　ā、ii、ū、ei（ē）、ō

　　　例　tokei、onēsan

3）文は分かち書きとした。原則として助詞は離したが、助詞を取り込んで1語と認められる語は分かち書きをしない。

例　nanika、desukara

4）接頭語、接尾語、助数詞のほか、複合語などをハイフンでつないだ。

例　o-shigoto、Tanaka-san、25-sai

　　hana-ya、benkyō-shimasu

ただし、上記の内でも、造語性が弱いもの、また1語として数えたいものにはハイフンを用いない。

例　hitotsu、hitori、ocha、asagohan、oyasuminasai

5）文頭、および固有名詞とその複合語などの語頭に大文字を用いた。

6）外国人の名前は、その国で用いられている慣用的ローマ字表記に従った。

7）外来語の一部は原音に近い表記をした。

例　pātii、fōku

4．その他

1）文中省略できる語句は［　　　］でくくった。

例　Hai、［watashi wa］Rao desu.

2）1つのものに違った表現がある場合はそれを（　　　）でくくって示した。

例　otearai (toire)

3）別の語句と置き換えができる部分は【　　　】でくくって示した。

例　【Kōhii】wa ikaga desu ka.

学習者のみなさんへ

1．言葉をよく覚え、文型を繰り返し練習しましょう。

　この教科書の分冊には各課ごとに新しい言葉が提出されています。まず、その言葉をよく覚えましょう。その上で、文型の正しい意味を捕らえ、文の形がしっかり身につくまで繰り返し練習してください。特に「練習Ａ，Ｂ」は実際に声を出して練習しましょう。

2．会話の練習を十分にしましょう。

　文型練習の次は会話練習です。「会話」には日常生活で遭遇するさまざまな場面を取り上げました。こうした会話に慣れるために、まず「練習Ｃ」でよく練習しましょう。それから「会話」で場面や状況にふさわしいやり取りのコツを覚えましょう。

3．テープを何度も聞きましょう。

　文型練習や会話練習の際は、正しい発音や抑揚などを身につけるために、テープを聞きながら、実際に声を出して練習しましょう。また、日本語の音やスピードに慣れ、内容を聞き取る力を養うためにも、テープを何度も聞きましょう。

4．必ず練習をしましょう。

　授業で習ったことを忘れないためにも、必ずその日のうちに復習をしましょう。最後に「問題」で学んだことを確認し、聞き取りの力試しをしましょう。

5．実際に話してみましょう。

　教室の中だけが学習の場ではありません。学んだ日本語を使って友達や一般の日本人に話しかけてみましょう。学んだものが役立てば、学習の励みにもなるでしょう。

　以上のことを守って、この教科書の勉強を終えると、日常生活に必要な基本的な語彙と日本語の基本的な表現が身につきます。焦らず根気よく勉強を続けてください。

Nihon no chizu

TKC (Tōkyō Kenshū Sentā)

Shinjuku

Ginza

YKC (Yokohama Kenshū Sentā)

Yokohama

Hokkaidō

Tōkyō

Honshū

Kyōto

Kōbe

Hiroshima

Fujisan

CKC (Chūbu Kenshū Sentā)

Shikoku

Nagoya

Kyūshū

Nara

Ōsaka

Okinawa

KKC (Kansai Kenshū Sentā)

Ōsakajō

Kono tekisuto no omona tōjō jinbutsu

- Sentā de Nihon-go o benkyō-shite iru kenshūsei

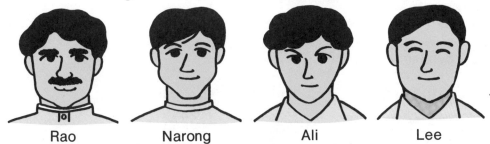

Rao   Narong   Ali   Lee

- Sentā ni sunde kaisha de jisshū-shite iru kenshūsei

Han   Kim   Mario

- Sentā de hataraite iru Nihon-jin

Tanaka	Kimura	Suzuki
Kōsu tantōsha	Uketsuke no hito	Nihon-go no sensei

- Sonota no hitobito

Katō   Satō   Hayashi   Yamamoto

Mokuji

pēji

I . **Nihon-go no hatsuon** ·· 1

II . **Kyōshitsu no kotoba** ·· 3

III . **Aisatsu** ·· 3

IV . **Sūji** ·· 3

Dai 1 ka ·· 4
  1. Watashi wa Rao desu.
  2. Narong-san wa Nihon-jin dewa arimasen.
  3. Ali-san wa kenshūsei desu ka.
  4. Lee-san mo kenshūsei desu.
  Kaiwa : Shōkai

Dai 2 ka ·· 12
  1. Kore wa hon desu.
  2. Sore wa watashi no hon desu.
  3. Kono hon wa watashi no desu.
  Kaiwa : Uketsuke de

Dai 3 ka ·· 20
  1. Koko wa kyōshitsu desu.
  2. Jimusho wa asoko desu.
  Kaiwa : Depāto de

Dai 4 ka ·· 28
  1. Ima 1-ji 10-pun desu.
  2. Watashi wa asa 6-ji ni okimasu.
  3. Watashi wa 9-ji kara 5-ji made hatarakimasu.
  4. Watashi wa kinō benkyō-shimashita.
  Kaiwa : Sukejūru

Dai 5 ka ·· 36
  1. Watashi wa Kyōto e ikimasu.
  2. Watashi wa hikōki de kuni e kaerimasu.
  3. Watashi wa tomodachi to Nihon e kimashita.
  Kaiwa : Densha ni noru

Dai 6 ka ··· 44
1. Watashi wa kōhii o nomimasu.
2. Watashi wa depāto de shatsu o kaimasu.
3. Issho ni gohan o tabemasen ka.
4. Robii de yasumimashō.
Kaiwa : Eiga ni iku

Fukushū A ·· 52

Dai 7 ka ··· 54
1. Watashi wa hashi de gohan o tabemasu.
2. Watashi wa Lee-san ni tokei o agemasu.
3. Watashi wa Tanaka-san ni jisho o moraimashita.
Kaiwa : Purezento

Dai 8 ka ··· 62
1. Rao-san wa shinsetsu desu.
2. Tōkyō wa ōkii desu.
3. Rao-san wa shinsetsuna hito desu.
4. Tōkyō wa ōkii machi desu.
Kaiwa : Sentā hōmon

Dai 9 ka ··· 70
1. Watashi wa ringo ga suki desu.
2. Watashi wa kamera ga arimasu.
3. Watashi wa onaka ga itai desu kara, byōin e ikimasu.
Kaiwa : Byōki

Dai 10 ka ··· 78
1. Jimusho ni Tanaka-san ga imasu.
2. Robii ni terebi ga arimasu.
3. Rao-san wa heya ni imasu.
4. Hon wa tsukue no ue ni arimasu.
Kaiwa : Michi o kiku

Dai 11 ka ··· 86
 1. Ringo o mittsu kaimasu.
 2. Konpyūtā ga 2-dai arimasu.
 3. Rao-san wa Nihon ni 1-nen imasu.
 Kaiwa : Yūbinkyoku de

Dai 12 ka ··· 94
 1. Kinō wa ame deshita.
 2. Kinō wa samukatta desu.
 3. Tōkyō wa Ōsaka yori ōkii desu.
 4. Kurasu de Narong-san ga ichiban wakai desu.
 Kaiwa : Ryokō

Dai 13 ka ··· 102
 1. Watashi wa kamera ga hoshii desu.
 2. Watashi wa eiga o mitai desu.
 3. Watashi wa depāto e kutsu o kai ni ikimasu.
 Kaiwa : Gaishutsu

Fukushū B ··· 110

Dai 14 ka ··· 112
 1. Jisho o kashite kudasai.
 2. Lee-san wa ima terebi o mite imasu.
 Kaiwa : Kamera-ya de

Dai 15 ka ··· 120
 1. Tabako o sutte mo ii desu.
 2. Rao-san wa ii kamera o motte imasu.
 Kaiwa : Kazoku

Dai 16 ka ··· 128
 1. Asa okite, gohan o tabete, kaisha e ikimasu.
 2. Shigoto ga owatte kara, sugu uchi e kaerimasu.
 3. Tōkyō wa hito ga ōkute, nigiyaka desu.
 Kaiwa : Resutoran e iku

Dai 17 ka ··· 136
1. Shashin o toranai de kudasai.
2. Mainichi benkyō-shinakereba narimasen.
3. Do-yōbi no gogo benkyō-shinakute mo ii desu.
Kaiwa : Kōjō-kengaku

Dai 18 ka ··· 144
1. Lee-san wa kanji o yomu koto ga dekimasu.
2. Watashi no shumi wa eiga o miru koto desu.
3. Neru mae ni, hon o yomimasu.
Kaiwa : Sukii

Dai 19 ka ··· 152
1. Nihon-ryōri o tabeta koto ga arimasu.
2. Nichi-yōbi kaimono-shitari, eiga o mitari shimasu.
3. Korekara dandan samuku narimasu.
Kaiwa : Hōmon

Fukushū C ··· 160

Dai 20 ka ··· 162
1. Ashita Tōkyō e iku.
2. Mainichi isogashii.
3. Kyō wa ii tenki da.
Kaiwa : Pātii

Dai 21 ka ··· 170
1. Konban ame ga furu to omoimasu.
2. Kaisha no hito wa ashita Sentā e kuru to iimashita.
Kaiwa : Kaigi

Dai 22 ka ··· 178
1. Kore wa watashi ga totta shashin desu.
2. Asoko ni iru hito wa Lee-san desu.
Kaiwa : Shigoto no ato de

Fukushū D ··· 186

Dai 23 ka ·· 188
  1. Gaikoku e iku toki, pasupōto ga irimasu.
  2. Kono botan o osu to, kikai ga ugokimasu.
Kaiwa : Jidō-kenbaiki

Dai 24 ka ·· 196
  1. Kimura-san wa watashi ni nekutai o kuremashita.
  2. Watashi wa Kimura-san ni kasa o kashite agemashita.
  3. Watashi wa Suzuki-san ni Nihon-go o oshiete moraimashita.
  4. Kanai wa watashi ni kodomo no shashin o okutte kuremashita.
Kaiwa : Nihon-go no benkyō

Dai 25 ka ·· 206
  1. Ame ga futtara, ikimasen.
  2. Ame ga futte mo, ikimasu.
Kaiwa : Ippan-kenshū ga owatte

Fukushū E ·· 216

Joshi ·· 218

Fōmu no tsukai-kata ·· 222

Fukushi, Fukushi-teki hyōgen ·································· 224

Setsuzoku no iroiro ·· 226

Sakuin ·· 227

Ⅰ. **Nihon-go no hatsuon**

    1.   Nihon-go no onsetsu

a	i	u	e	o
ka	ki	ku	ke	ko
sa	shi	su	se	so
ta	chi	tsu	te	to
na	ni	nu	ne	no
ha	hi	fu	he	ho
ma	mi	mu	me	mo
ya	(i)	yu	(e)	yo
ra	ri	ru	re	ro
wa	(i)	(u)	(e)	(o)
n				

kya	kyu	kyo
sha	shu	sho
cha	chu	cho
nya	nyu	nyo
hya	hyu	hyo
mya	myu	myo
rya	ryu	ryo

ga	gi	gu	ge	go
za	ji	zu	ze	zo
da	(ji)	(zu)	de	do
ba	bi	bu	be	bo
pa	pi	pu	pe	po

gya	gyu	gyo
ja	ju	jo
bya	byu	byo
pya	pyu	pyo

vowel

short   _long_

2. Tanboin to Chōboin

a   i   u   e   o   _double vowel in Romaji_

ā   ii   ū   ē, ei   ō   _or — sign above vowel_
                              = long sound.

obasan : obāsan   e : ē   koko : kōkō

ojisan : ojiisan   heya : heiya   toru : tōru

yuki : yūki   _In hiragana it is written with_
                  extra vowel hiragana.

3. Nijū shiin (Sokuon)   _Double consonant._

oto : otto   _① first cons. becomes 'a little' っ tsu._

kako : kakko   _② Sound is cut, pronounced with_
                  a break between cons.'s

isai : issai

kippu, motto, matchi

2

4. Shiin + ya, yu, yo (Yōon)   _Minimal pairs._

hiyaku : hyaku

riyū   : ryū

biyōin : byōin

kyaku, nyūsu, ryokō

5. "za, zu, zo" to "ja, ju, jo"

zāzā : jājā

kazu : kaju

kōzō : kōjō

6. "su" to "tsu"

chair isu   : itsu _when._

suki   : tsuki

Suzuki : tsuzuki

tsukue, atsui, kyōshitsu

classroom language

II. Kyōshitsu no kotoba

1. Hajimemashō. *Let's begin.*   8. namae, heya no bangō
2. Owarimashō. *Let's finish.*   9. shiken, shukudai *test homework.*
3. Yasumimashō. *break* 10. shitsumon, kotae, rei *question answer.*
4. Wakarimasu ka. *Do you understand?*

   はっキり = clearly *ha k ki ri*

   ···Hai, wakarimasu.

   ゆっくり *yu k ku ri = slowly*

   ···Iie, wakarimasen.

5. Mō ichido. *time Once more/one more time.* いって ください *itt te ku da sa i*
6. Kekkō desu. *that's right.*
7. Dame desu. *that's wrong*

SUBJECT PARTICLE OF SUB. OBJECT POSITIVE I (TO BE) ? ↓QUESTION.

$$ \boxed{A} \quad は \quad \boxed{B} \quad で す \quad \boxed{カ} 。 $$
wa   de s(u) ka

III. Aisatsu

1. Ohayō gozaimasu. NB SAME WORD ORDER FOR POS. & Q.

2. Konnichiwa.

   $$ \boxed{A} \quad は \quad \boxed{B} \quad で は \quad あ り ま せ ん $$
   de wa a ri ma sen

3. Konbanwa.
4. Oyasuminasai.   ↑ NEG.
5. Sayōnara.

   POSSESSIVE MY NAME わたし の なまえ
   watashi no namae
   I 's name

   YOUR NAME あなた の なまえ
   anata no namae
   You 's name

IV. Sūji

0 ··· zero, rei

1 ··· ichi   6 ··· roku

2 ··· ni   7 ··· nana, shichi

3 ··· san   8 ··· hachi   くに = country.
                                        ku ni
4 ··· yon, shi   9 ··· kyū, ku

5 ··· go   10 ··· jū

3

Dai 1 ka

STRUCTURES

Bunkei   particle of subject

1. Watashi wa Rao desu.

2. Narong-san wa Nihon-jin dewa arimasen.

    (ja) — conversational pronunc

3. Ali-san wa kenshūsei desu ka.

4. Lee-san mo kenshūsei desu.

    also (particle)

Reibun EXAMPLE.

1. Anata wa Rao-san desu ka.

    ···Hai, [watashi wa] Rao desu.

    ···Iie, [watashi wa] Rao dewa arimasen.

4

2. Narong-san wa Indoneshia-jin desu ka.

    ···Iie, Indoneshia-jin dewa arimasen.   Tai-jin desu.

3. Mario-san mo Tai-jin desu ka.

    ···Iie, Mario-san wa Firipin-jin desu.

4. Ano hito wa dare desu ka.

    ···Rao-san desu.

5. Rao-san wa kenshūsei desu ka.

    ···Hai, Tōkyō-denki no kenshūsei desu.

6. Tanaka-san wa nan-sai desu ka.

    ···28 [-sai] desu.

Kaiwa Conversation

<h2 style="text-align:center">Shōkai (INTRODUCTION).</h2>

Tanaka : Minasan, ohayō gozaimasu.

Watashi wa Tanaka desu.

Dōzo yoroshiku. – How do you do?

Rao : Hajimemashite.

Watashi wa Indo no Rao desu.

Tōkyō-denki no kenshūsei desu.

Senmon wa konpyūtā desu.

Dōzo yoroshiku.

5

which どの
どれ

THIS	だれ = who.
この	
THE + Noun.	なに = what
その ひと	(ん)
THAT. (person).	どの = or which
あの	(どれ)

Renshū A

1. Watashi wa   Rao   desu.
わたし は   Indo-jin   です
     kenshūsei

2. Watashi wa   Tanaka   dewa arimasen.
わたし は   Nihon-jin   でわ ありません
     sensei

3. Ano hito wa   Kimura-san   desu ka.
あの ひと は   Lee-san   です か
     Han-san
     dare (donata)

4. Watashi   mo kenshūsei desu.
Ano hito   も けんしゅうせい です
Narong-san

5. Ano hito wa   Indo   no   Rao-san   desu.
あの ひと は   Chūgoku   の   kenshūsei   です
     Tōkyō-denki   Katō-san

6. Ano hito wa   21-sai   desu.
あの ひと は   35-sai   です
     49-sai
     nan-sai (o-ikutsu)   ⋯⋯ ka.
              か

1

れんしゅう
Renshū B

1. Rei : watashi wa Nihon-jin desu ……Watashi wa Nihon-jin dewa arimasen.
   1) watashi wa Tanaka desu …… わたし は たなか でわ ありません。
   2) watashi-tachi wa Nihon-jin desu …… わたしたち は にほんじん でわありません。
   3) Tanaka-san wa sensei desu …… たなか さん は せんせい でわ ありません。 **1**
   4) ano hito wa kenshūsei desu …… あの ひと は けんしゅうせい でわ ありません。

2. Rei : Anata wa kenshūsei desu ka. ……Hai, kenshūsei desu.
   1) Rao-san wa Indo-jin desu ka. …… はい、<u>じんど</u>じん です。 } should be
   2) Narong-san wa Tai-jin desu ka. …… はい、<u>たじ</u>じん です。 } Katakana
   3) Minasan wa kenshūsei desu ka. …… はい、けんしゅうせい です。
   4) Suzuki-san wa sensei desu ka. …… はい、せんせい です。

3. Rei : Tanaka-san wa sensei desu ka. ……Iie, sensei dewa arimasen.
   1) Kim-san wa Nihon-jin desu ka. …… いいえ、にほんじん です ありません。
   2) Ano hito wa Tai-jin desu ka.…… いいえ、Tai じん です ありません。 <u>7</u>
   3) Lee-san wa Kankoku no kenshūsei desu ka. ……いいえ、かんこく の けんしゅうせい
   4) Ali-san wa Tōkyō-denki no kenshūsei desu ka. …… でわありません。
      いいえ、とうきょう でんき の けんしゅうせい でわ ありません。

4. Rei 1 : Anata mo kenshūsei desu ka. (hai)
      ……Hai, watashi mo kenshūsei desu.
   Rei 2 : Anata mo Indo-jin desu ka. (iie)
      ……Iie, watashi wa Indo-jin dewa arimasen.
   1) Rao-san <u>mo</u> kenshūsei desu ka. (hai) …… はい、も けんしゅうせい です。
   2) Anata mo Nihon-jin desu ka. (iie) …… いいえ、わたしも にほんじん でわありません。
   3) Suzuki-san mo sensei desu ka. (hai) …… はい、も せんせい です。
   4) Rao-san mo Nagoya-jidōsha no kenshūsei desu ka. (iie) …… いいえ、も なごやじどうしゃ
      の けんしゅうせい でわ ありません。
      ↑
   MO → particle must follow a noun
   cannot begin a sentence

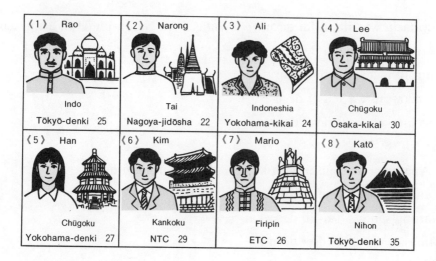

《1》 Rao	《2》 Narong	《3》 Ali	《4》 Lee
Indo	Tai	Indoneshia	Chūgoku
Tōkyō-denki 25	Nagoya-jidōsha 22	Yokohama-kikai 24	Ōsaka-kikai 30
《5》 Han	《6》 Kim	《7》 Mario	《8》 Katō
Chūgoku	Kankoku	Firipin	Nihon
Yokohama-denki 27	NTC 29	ETC 26	Tōkyō-denki 35

5. Rei : Rao-san wa Marēshia-jin desu ka. 《1》 ······Iie, Indo-jin desu.

☞ 1) Narong-san wa Indoneshia-jin desu ka. 《2》 ······

2) Ali-san mo Tai-jin desu ka. 《3》 ······

3) Lee-san wa Tōkyō-denki no kenshūsei desu ka. 《4》 ······

4) Han-san mo Ōsaka-kikai no kenshūsei desu ka. 《5》 ······

6. Rei : Ano hito wa dare desu ka. 《4》 ······Chūgoku no Lee-san desu.

☞ 1) Ano hito wa dare desu ka. 《5》 ······

2) Ano hito wa dare desu ka. 《6》 ······

3) Ano hito wa dare desu ka. 《7》 ······

4) Ano hito wa dare desu ka. 《8》 ······

7. Rei : Rao-san wa nan-sai desu ka. 《1》 ······25-sai desu.

☞ 1) Narong-san wa nan-sai desu ka. 《2》 ······

2) Ali-san wa nan-sai desu ka. 《3》 ······

3) Lee-san wa nan-sai desu ka. 《4》 ······

4) Han-san wa nan-sai desu ka. 《5》 ······

Renshū C

1. A : Hajimemashite.　Watashi wa <u>Rao</u> desu.
   　　　 Dōzo yoroshiku.
   B : Watashi wa Ali desu.
   　　　 Dōzo yoroshiku.

   　　 1） Lee
   　　 2） Han
   　　 3） Mario

2. A : Rao-san wa Indo-jin desu ka.
   B : Hai, Indo-jin desu.
   A : Ano hito mo Indo-jin desu ka.
   B : Iie, ano hito wa <u>Tai-jin</u> desu.

   　　 1） Indoneshia-jin
   　　 2） Firipin-jin
   　　 3） Marēshia-jin

3. A : Ano hito wa dare desu ka.
   B : <u>Ali-san</u> desu.
   　　 ①
   　　 <u>Yokohama-kikai</u> no kenshūsei desu.
   　　 ②

   　　 1） ① Rao　　② Tōkyō-denki
   　　 2） ① Han　　② Yokohama-denki
   　　 3） ① Lee　　② Ōsaka-kikai

Mondai

1. Rei : <u>Iie, watashi wa sensei dewa arimasen.</u>

   🔊 1) _____

   2) _____

   3) _____

   4) _____

   5) _____

2.

🔊 Rei : Rao-san wa $\left\{\begin{array}{l}\text{a. 22-sai}\\ \text{b. 25-sai}\\ \text{c. 29-sai}\end{array}\right\}$ desu.

1) Narong-san wa $\left\{\begin{array}{l}\text{a. Nihon-jin}\\ \text{b. Indo-jin}\\ \text{c. Tai-jin}\end{array}\right\}$ desu.

2) Suzuki-san wa $\left\{\begin{array}{l}\text{a. Nihon-jin}\\ \text{b. Chūgoku-jin}\\ \text{c. Kankoku-jin}\end{array}\right\}$ desu.

3) Ano hito wa $\left\{\begin{array}{l}\text{a. Yokohama-kikai no Katō-san}\\ \text{b. Tōkyō-denki no Tanaka-san}\\ \text{c. Tōkyō-denki no Katō-san}\end{array}\right\}$ desu.

4) Lee-san wa $\left\{\begin{array}{l}\text{a. Ōsaka-kikai}\\ \text{b. Yokohama-kikai}\\ \text{c. Nagoya-jidōsha}\end{array}\right\}$ no kenshūsei desu.

5) Kim-san wa $\left\{\begin{array}{l}\text{a. Chūgoku-jin}\\ \text{b. Kankoku-jin}\\ \text{c. Nihon-jin}\end{array}\right\}$ desu.

3. Rei : (13)

🔊 a) (26)   f) (41)   k) (51)

   b) (5)   g) (68)   l) (20)

   c) (15)   h) (98)   m) (12)

   d) (30)   i) (60)   n) (41)

   e) (13)   j) (16)   o) (8)

4. Rei : Anata wa (kenshūsei) desu ka. ······Hai, kenshūsei desu.

    1) Anata wa (Lee-san) desu ka. ······Hai, watashi wa Lee desu.

    2) Tanaka-san wa (sensei) desu ka. ······Iie, sensei dewa arimasen.

    3) Narong-san wa (Indo-jin) desu ka.

        ······Iie, Indo-jin dewa arimasen.   Tai-jin desu.

    4) Ano hito wa (dare) desu ka. ······Indo no Rao-san desu. (donata)

    5) Ali-san wa (nan-sai) desu ka. ······24-sai desu. (o-ikutsu)

1

5. Rei : Narong / watashi / desu / wa

        ······Watashi wa Narong desu.   わたし は Narong です

    1) dewa arimasen / ano hito / wa / kenshūsei

        ······ Ano hito wa kenshūsei   あの ひと は けんしゅうせい でも ありません
        dewa arimasen.

    2) desu / no / Han / Chūgoku / wa / watashi

        ······ watashi wa Chūgoku no Han desu.
        わたし は ちゅうごく の Han です

    3) o-ikutsu / ka / desu / wa / sensei

        ······ sensei wa o-ikutsu desu ka
        せんせい は おいくつ です か

    11

    4) Katō-san / wa / ano hito / desu / no / Tōkyō-denki

        ······ ano hito wa Tōkyō-denki の Katō-san desu.
        あの ひと は とうきょう でんき の かとう さん です

Introductions.

6. [Shōkai]

    Hajimemashite.

    Watashi wa (   ) no (   ) desu.

    (   ) no kenshūsei desu.

    Senmon wa (   ) desu.

    Dōzo (   ).

と = and.   つぎ = next.

よう の ⎰ use for
yo no ⎱

Dai 2 ka
lesson.

sentence pattern
Bunkei

1. Kore wa hon desu.　これ は ほん です。

2. Sore wa watashi no hon desu.　それ は わたし の ほん です。

3. Kono hon wa watashi no desu.　この ほん は わたし の です。

Example sentence.
Reibun

1. Kore wa jisho desu ka.　これ は じしょ です か。
   …Hai, sō desu.　…… はい、そう です。

2. Sore wa enpitsu desu ka.　それ は えんぴつ です か。
   …Iie, sō dewa arimasen.　　Bōrupen desu.
   …… いいえ、そう でわ ありません。ぼ"うるぺん です。

3. Sore wa nan desu ka.　それ は なん です か。
   …[Kore wa] raitā desu.　[これ は] ライター です。

4. それ は ボールペン です か、シャープ ペンシル です か。
   Sore wa bōrupen desu ka, shāpu-penshiru desu ka.
   …Shāpu-penshiru desu.　*repeat after every choice.*
   …… シャープ ペンシル です。

5. Are wa dare no kaban desu ka.　あれ は だれ の かばん です か。
   …Lee-san no kaban desu. ……　Lee-さん の かばん です。

6. Kono jisho wa anata no desu ka.　この じしょ は あなた の です か。
   …Iie, watashi no dewa arimasen. ……いいえ、わたし の でわ ありません。

7. Kono hon wa dare no desu ka.　この ほん は だれ の です か。
   …Watashi no desu.　…… わたし の です。

つぎ の
next (particle)

Conversation
Kaiwa

Reception
Uketsuke de → particle of place 'at'

Rao   : 308 onegai-shimasu. (asking for help or a favour)

Kimura : Hai, dōzo.

Kore wa anata no tegami desu ka.

Rao   : Hai, sō desu.

Dōmo arigatō gozaimasu.

Kimura : A, chotto matte kudasai.

Kono bōrupen mo anata no desu ka.

Rao   : Iie, chigaimasu.

ちがいます / ちがう
wrong ! mas   base form

☐ は えいご で なん ですか。
what is ☐ in English ?

Renshū A

1. Kore wa   jisho   desu.
             shinbun
             haizara
             nan   ...... ka.

2. Sore wa   hon   desu ka,   jisho   desu ka.
             rajio   tēpu-rekōdā
             enpitsu   bōrupen

3. Are wa   watashi   no kaban desu.
            Kimura-san
            Rao-san
            dare   .... ka.

4. Kore wa   watashi   no desu.
             Kimura-san
             Rao-san
             dare   .... ka.

5. Kono   hon   wa watashi no desu.
           nōto
           kaban

2

14

Renshū B

ANSWERS ONLY.

example

1. Rei 1 : Kore wa kagi desu ka.

   ……Hai, sō desu. Kagi desu. … はい、そうです。かぎです。

   Rei 2 : Kore wa hon desu ka.

   ……Iie, sō dewa arimasen. Jisho desu. … いいえ、そうでわありません。じしょです。

   1) Kore wa kami desu ka. …… はい、そうです。かみです。

   2) Kore wa hako desu ka. …… いいえ、そうでわありません。かばんです。

   3) Kore wa tēpu-rekōdā desu ka. …… はい、そうです。テープレコーターです。

   4) Kore wa mado desu ka. …… いいえ、そうでわありません。と です。
   （ドア）

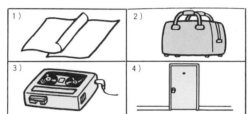

と = door
ドア = "

2

15

2. Rei : Are wa nan desu ka.

   ……Tokei desu.

   1) Are wa nan desu ka. ……いすです。

   2) Are wa nan desu ka. …… つくえ です。

   3) Are wa nan desu ka. …… でんわ です。

   4) Are wa nan desu ka. …… テレビ です。

3. Rei 1 : Kore wa anata no bōrupen desu ka. (hai)

   ……Hai, watashi no bōrupen desu. はい、わたしの ボールペン です。

   Rei 2 : Kore wa anata no hon desu ka. (iie)

   ……Iie, watashi no hon dewa arimasen. いいえ、わたし の ほん でわ ありません。

   1) Kore wa anata no tabako desu ka. (hai) …… はわたしの たばこ です。

   2) Kore wa anata no rajio desu ka. (iie) …… いいえ、わたしの ラジオ でわ ありません。

   3) Kore wa Rao-san no nōto desu ka. (hai) …… はい、ラオさんの ノート です。

   4) Kore wa sensei no jisho desu ka. (iie) …… いいえ、せんせいの じしょ でわ ありません。

よんで = read　　　いっしょに = together
こたえて = answer

4.　Rei :　Kore wa dare no hon desu ka. (watashi) ……Watashi no hon desu.

　　1）　Kore wa dare no kamera desu ka. (Lee-san) …Lee～さん の カメラ です。

　　2）　Sore wa dare no kagi desu ka. (Narong-san) Narong～さんの かぎ です。

　　3）　Are wa dare no kaban desu ka. (sensei) …せんせいの かばん です。

　　4）　Kore wa dare no tabako desu ka. (Ali-san) …Ali～さん の たばこ です。

5.　Rei 1 :　Kore wa Rao-san no desu ka. (hai) ……Hai, Rao-san no desu.

　　Rei 2 :　Sore wa Ali-san no desu ka. (iie) ……Iie, Ali-san no dewa arimasen.

　　1）　Kore wa Narong-san no desu ka. (hai) はい、Narong～さん の です。

　　2）　Sore wa Lee-san no desu ka. (iie) いいえ、Lee～さん の でわ ありません。

　　3）　Kore wa Tanaka-san no desu ka. (hai) はい、Tanaka-さん の です。

　　4）　Sore wa Kimura-san no desu ka. (iie) いいえ、Kimura～さん の でわ
　　　　　　　　　　　　　　　　　　　　　　　　　　　ありません。

6.　Rei :　Kono zasshi [magazine] wa dare no desu ka. (Narong-san)
　　　　……Narong-san no desu. Narong さん の です。

　　1）　Kono shāpu-penshiru wa dare no desu ka. (Ali-san) Ali さん の です。

　　2）　Sono matchi wa dare no desu ka. (Rao-san) …Rao さん の です。

　　3）　Ano jidōsha [automobile] wa dare no desu ka. (Tanaka-san) Tanaka さん の です。

　　4）　Kono kaban wa dare no desu ka. (Katō-san) …Katō-さん の です。

7.　Rei :　Kono jisho wa Narong-san no desu ka, Ali-san no desu ka.
　　　　(Ali-san) ……Ali-san no desu.

　　1）　Kono kaban wa Lee-san no desu ka, Han-san no desu ka.
　　　　(Lee-san) ……Lee さん の です。

　　2）　Sono kamera wa Kim-san no desu ka, Mario-san no desu ka.
　　　　(Mario-san) ……Mario-さん の です。

　　3）　Ano jidōsha wa Kimura-san no desu ka, Tanaka-san no desu ka.
　　　　(Kimura-san) ……Kimura-さん の です。

　　4）　Kono hon wa Rao-san no desu ka, Narong-san no desu ka.
　　　　(Narong-san) ……Narong さん の です。

2

16

Renshū C

1. A : Kore wa anata no <u>kaban</u> desu ka.

    B : Hai, sō desu.

         Dōmo arigatō gozaimasu.

    1) nōto
    2) bōrupen
    3) jisho

2. A : Kono hon wa anàta no desu ka.

    B : Iie, chigaimasu.   <u>Narong-san</u> no desu.

    1) Ali-san
    2) Tanaka-san
    3) sensei

3. A : Kono <u>kamera</u> wa dare no desu ka.

    B : Watashi no desu.

         Dōmo arigatō gozaimasu.

    1) tokei
    2) kagi
    3) raitā

Mondai

1.

1) これ は ライタ です。
2) これ は ざっし です。
3) これ は えんぴつ です。
4) これ は Rao さん の かばん です。
5) これ は Narong さん の ほん です。

2.

1) Kore wa { a. rajio / b. terebi / c. tēpu-rekōdā } desu.

2) Kono kamera wa { a. watashi / b. Ali-san / c. Tanaka-san } no desu.

3) Kono hon wa { a. Ali-san / b. Narong-san / c. Lee-san } no desu.

4) Kono kagi wa { a. watashi / b. Rao-san / c. Ali-san } no desu.

5) Watashi no kagi wa { a. 426 / b. 427 / c. 428 } desu.

3. Rei : Ano hito wa (dare   ) desu ka. ······Chūgoku no Han-san desu.

1) Kore wa (haizara) desu ka. ······Hai, sō desu.   Haizara desu.

2) Sore wa (hon   ) desu ka. ······Iie, hon dewa arimasen.   Jisho desu.

3) Are wa (nan   ) desu ka. ······Tēpu-rekōdā desu.

4) Sore wa (bōrupen) desu ka, shāpu-penshiru desu ka.

······Bōrupen desu.

5) Kore wa (dare   ) no hon desu ka. ······Lee-san no hon desu.

6) Kono nōto mo (Lee-san) no desu ka.

······Iie, sore wa Lee-san no dewa arimasen.

7) Ano kamera wa (dare   ) no desu ka. ······Ali-san no desu.

8) Kono enpitsu wa (anata) no desu ka.

······Hai, sō desu.   Watashi no desu.

4. Rei : wa / shinbun / desu / kore

······Kore wa shinbun desu.

1) watashi / wa / sore / no / desu / kagi

······ Sore wa watashi no kagi desu.

2) no / desu / watashi / hon / kono / wa

······ Kono wa watashi no hon desu.

3) kaban / dewa arimasen / wa / ano / no / watashi

······ Ano kaban wa watashi no dewa arimasen.

4) tabako / no / dare / kono / wa / ka / desu

······ Kono wa dare no tabako desu ka.

5. Lee   : 516 (   ).

Kimura : Hai, dōzo.

Kore wa anata no tegami desu ka.

Lee   : Hai, sō desu.   Dōmo (   ).

Kimura : Kono shinbun mo anata no desu ka.

Lee   : Iie, (   ).

2

19

(COLLOQUIAL)

こっち = this ⎫ near
そっち = that ⎫ way
あっち = that ⎫ far
どっち = (which way?)

ここ = here
そこ = there
あそこ = there (over)
どこ = (where?)

Dai 3 ka

Bunkei

1. Koko wa kyōshitsu desu.

2. Jimusho wa asoko desu.

3

Reibun

1. Koko wa uketsuke desu ka.

   ···Iie, jimusho desu.

   おてら = temple = don't confuse!

2. Otearai wa doko desu ka.

   ···Asoko desu.

3. Rao-san wa doko desu ka.

   ···Heya desu.

   どっち = conversational

4. Shokudō wa dochira desu ka.

   ···Achira desu.

   what?

5. Kaisha wa dochira desu ka.

   ···NTC desu.

6. NTC wa nan no kaisha desu ka.

   ···Konpyūtā no kaisha desu.

7. Sore wa doko no tokei desu ka.

   ···Nihon no tokei desu.

8. Kono kamera wa ikura desu ka.

   ···38,000-en desu.

20

(POLITE)

こちら = this ⎫
そちら = that ⎬ way
あちら = that ⎭
どちら = (which way.

なんの [N] ⎫ what kind/sort
⎬ of
どんな [N] ⎭ (company/ school).

Kaiwa

Depāto de

Rao	:	Chotto sumimasen.
Ten'in A	:	Hai.

shop assistant
(member).

Rao	:	Kaban-uriba wa doko desu ka.

(place)

Ten'in A	:	Kaban-uriba desu ka. 5-kai desu.
Rao	:	Dōmo.

floor/story.

Ten'in B	:	Irasshaimase.

いらっしゃい (ませ) = without ませ you can welcome friends into your home

Rao	:	Kono kaban wa ikura desu ka.
Ten'in B	:	3,500-en desu.

21

Rao	:	Ja, kore o kudasai. (lit. give me / I'll have).

particle of subject.

トイレ = toilet.
to i re

おべんじょ = toilet

Renshū A

1. Koko wa | robii (lobby) | desu.
   kyōshitsu
   otearai

2. Jimusho wa | koko | desu.
   soko
   asoko
   doko ...... ka.

3. Narong-san wa | asoko | desu.
   uketsuke
   niwa (garden)
   doko ...... ka.

(dining hall)

4. Shokudō wa | kochira | desu.
   sochira
   achira
   dochira ...... ka.

5. Are wa | Nihon | no jidōsha desu.
   Amerika
   ATM
   doko .... ka.

6. Kono tokei wa | 5,500-en | desu.
   12,000-en
   38,400-en
   ikura ...... ka.

Renshū B

1. Rei : ······Otearai wa doko desu ka.
   ☞ 1) ······
      2) ······
      3) ······
      4) ······

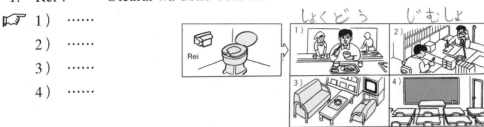

2. Rei : Haizara wa doko desu ka. (soko) ······ Soko desu.
   1) Denwa wa doko desu ka. (asoko) ······
   2) Terebi wa doko desu ka. (robii) ······
   3) Rao-san wa doko desu ka. (heya) ······
   4) Anata no uchi wa doko desu ka. (Yokohama) ······

3. Rei : ······Uketsuke wa dochira desu ka.
   ☞ 1) ······
      2) ······
      3) ······
      4) ······

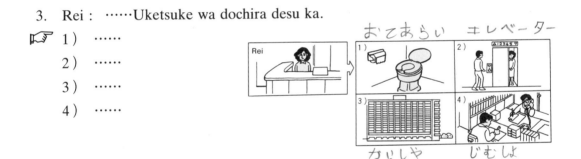

4. Rei : Narong-san no kuni wa dochira desu ka. (Tai) ······Tai desu.
   1) Anata no kaisha wa dochira desu ka. (NTC) ······
   2) Lee-san no kuni wa dochira desu ka. (Chūgoku) ······
   3) Ali-san no kuni wa dochira desu ka. (Indoneshia) ······
   4) Rao-san no kaisha wa dochira desu ka. (Tōkyō-denki) ······

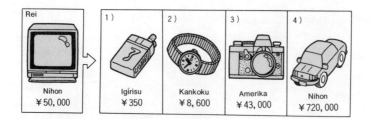

Rei	1)	2)	3)	4)
Nihon ¥50,000	Igírisu ¥350	Kankoku ¥8,600	Amerika ¥43,000	Nihon ¥720,000

5. Rei : Kore wa doko no terebi desu ka. ······Nihon no terebi desu.

 1) Kore wa doko no tabako desu ka. ······

2) Sore wa doko no tokei desu ka. ······

3) Sore wa doko no kamera desu ka. ······

4) Are wa doko no jidōsha desu ka. ······

6. Rei : Kono terebi wa ikura desu ka. ······50,000-en desu.

 1) Kono tabako wa ikura desu ka. ······

2) Kono tokei wa ikura desu ka. ······

3) Kono kamera wa ikura desu ka. ······

4) Kono jidōsha wa ikura desu ka. ······

Renshū C

1. A : Chotto sumimasen.
   Uketsuke wa doko desu ka.
   B : Asoko desu.
   A : Dōmo.

   1) otearai
   2) shokudō
   3) jimusho

2. A : Kaisha wa dochira desu ka.
   B : NTC desu.
        ①
   A : Nan no kaisha desu ka.
   B : Konpyūtā no kaisha desu.
        ②

   1) ① ATM   ② jidōsha
   2) ① Mirion   ② kamera
   3) ① ETC   ② erebētā

3. A : Kore wa doko no tokei desu ka.
                          ①
   B : Nihon no desu.
   A : Ikura desu ka.
   B : 5,000-en desu.
        ②
   A : Ja, kore o kudasai.

   1) ① kaban   ② 17,000-en
   2) ① tēpu-rekōdā   ② 23,600-en
   3) ① kamera   ② 42,800-en

Mondai

1. 1) _____

   📼 2) _____

   3) _____

   4) _____

   5) _____

2.

   📼 1) Jimusho wa $\begin{cases} \text{a. koko} \\ \text{b. soko} \\ \text{c. asoko} \end{cases}$ desu.

   2) Tanaka-san wa $\begin{cases} \text{a. kyōshitsu} \\ \text{b. jimusho} \\ \text{c. shokudō} \end{cases}$ desu.

   3) ATM wa $\begin{cases} \text{a. denki} \\ \text{b. jidōsha} \\ \text{c. kikai} \end{cases}$ no kaisha desu.

   4) Kamera-uriba wa $\begin{cases} \text{a. 1-kai} \\ \text{b. 5-kai} \\ \text{c. 6-kai} \end{cases}$ desu.

   5) Mirion no kamera wa $\begin{cases} \text{a. 58,300-en} \\ \text{b. 53,800-en} \\ \text{c. 38,500-en} \end{cases}$ desu.

3

26

3.

Rei : Koko wa (otearai) desu.

1) Koko wa (しょくどう) desu.   4) Koko wa (きょうしつ) desu.

2) Koko wa (じむしょ) desu.   5) Koko wa (にわ) desu.

3) Koko wa (へや) desu.

4. Rei : Sore wa [nan] desu ka. ······Raitā desu.

1) Sumimasen. Otearai wa [どちら] desu ka. ······Achira desu.

2) Rao-san wa [どこ] desu ka. ······Heya desu.

3) Narong-san no kuni wa [どちら] desu ka. ······Tai desu.

4) Kore wa [どこ] no tokei desu ka. ······Nihon no tokei desu.

5) Kono tokei wa [いくら] desu ka. ······15,000-en desu.

6) Tanaka-san wa [なんさい] desu ka. ······32-sai desu.
[おいくつ]

5. Rei : (Watashi, (Watashi wa), Watashi no) Indoneshia no Ali desu.

1) ((Kore), Kono, Koko) wa Igirisu no tabako desu.

2) (Sore, (Sono), Soko) kaban wa (watashi, watashi wa, (watashi no)) desu.

3) Otearai wa (are, ano, (asoko)) desu.

4) Sumimasen. Uketsuke wa (dare, nan, (doko)) desu ka.

27

Dai 4 ka

Bunkei

1. Ima 1-ji 10-pun desu. いま いちじ じゅっぷん です。

2. Watashi wa asa 6-ji ni okimasu. わたしは あさ ろくじ に おきます。

3. Watashi wa 9-ji kara 5-ji made hatarakimasu. わたしは きゅうじ からごじ まで はたらきます。

4. Watashi wa kinō benkyō-shimashita. わたしは きのう べんきょう しました。

Reibun

1. Ima nan-ji desu ka. いま なじ です か。

   ···4-ji 5-fun desu. よじ ごふん です。

2. Asa nan-ji ni okimasu ka. あさ なじ に おきます か。

   ···6-ji ni okimasu. ろくじ に おきます。

3. Mainichi nan-ji kara nan-ji made hatarakimasu ka. まいにち なんじ から なんじ まで はたらきます か

   ···8-ji kara 4-ji made hatarakimasu. はちじ からよじ まで はたらきます

4. Kōgi wa nan-ji kara desu ka. こうぎ は なんじ から です か。

   ···1-ji han kara desu. いちじ はん から です。

5. Ashita hatarakimasu ka. あした はたらきます か。

   ···Hai, hatarakimasu. はい、はたらきます。

   ···Iie, hatarakimasen. いいえ、はたらきません。

6. Kinō no ban benkyō-shimashita ka. きのうの ばん べんきょう しました か。

   ···Hai, benkyō-shimashita. はい、べんきょう しました。

   ···Iie, benkyō-shimasendeshita. いいえ しませんでした。 べんきょう

7. Kyō wa nan-yōbi desu ka. きょう は なんようび です か。

   ···Ka-yōbi desu. かようび です。

Kaiwa

Sukejūru

Katō :　Nihon-go no benkyō wa nan-ji kara desu ka.　にほんご の べんきょう は なんじ から です か。

Rao :　9-ji kara desu.　くじ から です。

Katō :　Nan-ji made desu ka.　なじ まで です か。

Rao :　12-ji made desu.　じゅう じ まで です。

Katō :　Sō desu ka.　そう です か。

　　　　Kyō no gogo wa nan desu ka.　きょう の ごご は なんです か。

Rao :　Kōgi desu.　こうぎ です。

Katō :　Nan-ji ni owarimasu ka.　なんじ に おわります か。

Rao :　5-ji ni owarimasu.　ごじ に おわります。

Katō :　Mainichi taihen desu ne.　まいにち たいへん です ね。

Renshū A

1. Ima   1-ji   desu.

            4-ji 5-fun

            9-ji han

            nan-ji   ······ ka.

2. Watashi wa asa   6-ji   ni okimasu.

                      6-ji han

                      7-ji han

    Anata wa   ···   nan-ji   ············· ka.

3. Watashi wa   9-ji   kara   5-ji   made hatarakimasu.

                   getsu-yōbi   kin-yōbi

                   asa   ban

4. Kōgi wa   1-ji   kara   4-ji   made desu.

              1-ji han   4-ji han

              2-ji   5-ji

              nan-ji   nan-ji   ············· ka.

5. Watashi wa   mainichi   benkyō-shimasu.

               ashita

               kinō   benkyō-shimashita.

               kinō no ban

6.

ne masu	ne masen	ne mashita	ne masendeshita
yasumi masu	yasumi masen	yasumi mashita	yasumi masendeshita
hataraki masu	hataraki masen	hataraki mashita	hataraki masendeshita
– I sleep	I don't sleep	I slept	I didn't sleep
– take a rest	don't take a rest	took a rest	didn't take a rest.
– work	not work	worked	didn't work.

Renshū B

1. Rei : Ima nan-ji desu ka. ······4-ji desu.
    ☞ 1) Ima nan-ji desu ka. ······
    2) Ima nan-ji desu ka. ······
    3) Ima nan-ji desu ka. ······
    4) Ima nan-ji desu ka. ······
    5) Ima nan-ji desu ka. ······

2. Rei : Maiban nan-ji ni nemasu ka. (10-ji) ······10-ji ni nemasu.
    1) Maiasa nan-ji ni okimasu ka. (6-ji) ······
    2) Maiasa nan-ji ni okimasu ka. (7-ji han) ······
    3) Maiban nan-ji ni nemasu ka. (12-ji) ······
    4) Maiban nan-ji ni nemasu ka. (11-ji han) ······

3. Rei : Ashita nan-ji kara nan-ji made benkyō-shimasu ka.
    ☞   ······9-ji kara 12-made benkyō-shimasu.
    1) Hiru nan-ji kara nan-ji made yasumimasu ka. ······
    2) Mainichi nan-ji kara nan-ji made hatarakimasu ka. ······
    3) Maiban nan-ji kara nan-ji made benkyō-shimasu ka. ······
    4) Do-yōbi nan-ji kara nan-ji made hatarakimasu ka. ······

4. Rei : Kōgi wa nan-ji kara desu ka. (2-ji) ······2-ji kara desu.

   1) Nihon-go no benkyō wa nan-ji kara desu ka. (9-ji) ······

   2) Kengaku wa nan-ji made desu ka. (4-ji han) ······

   3) Kaisha wa nan-ji kara nan-ji made desu ka. (8-ji, 4-ji) ······

   4) Shokudō wa hiru nan-ji kara nan-ji made desu ka. (12-ji, 1-ji han) ······

5. Rei 1 : Ashita yasumimasu ka. (hai) ······Hai, yasumimasu.

   Rei 2 : Ashita benkyō-shimasu ka. (iie) ······Iie, benkyō-shimasen.

   1) Konban benkyō-shimasu ka. (hai) ······

   2) Do-yōbi yasumimasu ka. (iie) ······

   3) Do-yōbi hatarakimasu ka. (hai) ······

   4) Nichi-yōbi benkyō-shimasu ka. (iie) ······

6. Rei : 9-ji ni nemasu (kinō no ban) ······Kinō no ban 9-ji ni nemashita.

   1) 9-ji kara benkyō-shimasu (kinō no ban) ······

   2) 6-ji ni okimasu (kesa) ······

   3) 12-ji made benkyō-shimasu (ototoi no ban) ······

   4) 7-ji made hatarakimasu (kinō) ······

7. Rei 1 : Kinō yasumimashita ka. (hai) ······Hai, yasumimashita.

   Rei 2 : Kinō benkyō-shimashita ka. (iie) ······Iie, benkyō-shimasendeshita.

   1) Kinō hatarakimashita ka. (hai) ······

   2) Kinō no ban benkyō-shimashita ka. (iie) ······

   3) Kesa benkyō-shimashita ka. (hai) ······

   4) Nichi-yōbi yasumimashita ka. (iie) ······

Renshū C

1. A : Mainichi nan-ji kara nan-ji made hatarakimasu ka.

   B : 9-ji kara 7-ji made hatarakimasu.
   ① ②

   A : Sō desu ka.　Taihen desu ne.

   1)　① 8-ji　　② 7-ji

   2)　① 9-ji　　② 6-ji

   3)　① 7-ji han　② 5-ji

2. A : Kyō no gogo wa nan desu ka.

   B : Kōgi desu.
   ①

   A : Nan-ji kara desu ka.

   B : 2-ji kara desu.
   ②

   1)　① kengaku　　　② 1-ji

   2)　① Nihon-go no benkyō　② 2-ji

   3)　① kōgi　　　② 1-ji han

3. A : Kinō benkyō-shimashita ka.

   B : Hai, 11-ji made benkyō-shimashita.
   ①

   A : Taihen desu ne.　Nan-ji ni nemashita ka.

   B : 12-ji ni nemashita.
   ②

   1)　① 12-ji　　② 1-ji

   2)　① 10-ji　　② 11-ji

   3)　① 12-ji han　② 1-ji

4

Mondai

1. 1) _____
   2) _____
   3) _____
   4) _____
   5) _____

2. 1) Ima ⎰ a. 1-ji han
            ⎱ b. 7-ji han ✓ ⎰ desu.
               c. 8-ji han

   2) Kōgi wa ⎰ a. 4-ji
              ⎱ b. 4-ji han ✓ ⎰ ni owarimasu.
                 c. 5-ji

   3) Kinō no ban ⎰ a. 7-ji kara 9-ji made
                  ⎱ b. 7-ji kara 10-ji made ⎰ benkyō-shimashita.
                     c. 8-ji kara 10-ji made ✓

   4) Kaisha wa ⎰ a. 7-ji kara 5-ji made ✓
                ⎱ b. 8-ji kara 5-ji made ⎰ desu.
                   c. 9-ji kara 5-ji made

   5) Watashi wa ⎰ a. getsu-yōbi kara do-yōbi made ✓
                 ⎱ b. getsu-yōbi kara kin-yōbi made ⎰ hatarakimasu.
                    c. getsu-yōbi kara moku-yōbi made

3. Rei : (③:00   5:00)
   1) (1:00 ✓   7:00)   5) (7:40 ✓   8:40)
   2) (4:10   4:40 ✓)   6) (1,980   1,098 ✓)
   3) (10:20   12:20 ✓)   7) (4,380 ✓   43,800)
   4) (9:15 ✓   9:30)

4.

Rei : nemasu	nemasen	nemashita	nemasendeshita
1)			
2)			
3)			
4)			

5. Rei : Kore wa [dare   ] (no   ) kaban desu ka. ······Lee-san no desu.

1) Ima [なんじ　　] desu ka. ······5-ji han desu.

2) Kinō no ban [なんじ　] (に) nemashita ka.
   ······10-ji ni nemashita.

3) Maiasa [なんじ　] (に) okimasu ka. ······7-ji ni okimasu.

4) Kōgi wa [なんじから] (から) desu ka. ······2-ji kara desu.

5) Nihon-go no benkyō wa [なんじ　] (まで) desu ka.
   ······12-ji made desu.

6) Mainichi [なんじ　] (から) [なじ　　] (まで) hatarakimasu ka.
   ······9-ji kara 5-ji made hatarakimasu.

7) Kyō no gogo wa [なん　　] desu ka. ······Kōgi desu.

8) Ashita wa [なん ようび] desu ka. ······Sui-yōbi desu.

おぼえて じます。 = to remember.

Dai 5 ka

Bunkei

1. Watashi wa Kyōto e ikimasu.
2. Watashi wa hikōki de kuni e kaerimasu.
3. Watashi wa tomodachi to Nihon e kimashita.

Reibun

1. Ashita doko e ikimasu ka.

   ···Kyōto e ikimasu.

2. Kinō doko e ikimashita ka.

   ···Doko [e] mo ikimasendeshita.

3. Nan de Kyōto e ikimasu ka.

   ···Shinkansen de ikimasu.

4. Dare to Sentā e kimashita ka.

   ···Katō-san to kimashita.

5. Itsu Nihon e kimashita ka.

   ···9-gatsu ni kimashita.

   Itsu kuni e kaerimasu ka.

   ···Rainen kaerimasu.

6. Tanjōbi wa nan-gatsu nan-nichi desu ka.

   ···3-gatsu 15-nichi desu.

Kaiwa

Densha ni noru

Rao	:	Sumimasen. Yokohama made ikura desu ka.
Onna no hito	:	300-en desu.
Rao	:	Dōmo.

Rao	:	A, Kimura-san, doko e ikimasu ka.
Kimura	:	Uchi e kaerimasu. Rao-san wa?
Rao	:	Tomodachi no uchi e ikimasu.
		Kono densha wa Yokohama e ikimasu ka.
Kimura	:	Iie, ikimasen. 3-bansen desu yo.
Rao	:	Sō desu ka. Arigatō.

Renshū A

1. Watashi wa   sūpā   e ikimasu.
                hon-ya
                Tōkyō
  Anata wa   doko   .... ka.

2. Watashi wa   basu   de Kyōto e ikimasu.
                densha
                shinkansen
  Anata wa   nan   .... ka.

3. Watashi wa   tomodachi   to Nihon e kimashita.
                Ali-san
                kaisha no hito
  Anata wa   dare   .... ka.

4. Watashi wa   ashita   kuni e kaerimasu.
                5-gatsu ni
                7-gatsu 18-nichi ni
  Anata wa   itsu   .... ka.

Renshū B

1. Rei : Ashita doko e ikimasu ka. (Yokohama) ······Yokohama e ikimasu.

   1) Nichi-yōbi doko e ikimasu ka. (depāto) ······
   2) Kinō doko e ikimashita ka. (Ginza) ······
   3) Kinō no ban doko e ikimashita ka. (tomodachi no uchi) ······
   4) Konban doko e ikimasu ka. (doko mo) ······

2. Rei : Nan de Tōkyō e ikimasu ka. ······Densha de ikimasu.

   1) Nan de kaisha e ikimasu ka. ······
   2) Nan de Sentā e kimashita ka. ······
   3) Nan de kuni e kaerimasu ka. ······
   4) Nan de ginkō e ikimashita ka. ······

3. Rei : Dare to kōjō e ikimasu ka. (Katō-san) ······Katō-san to ikimasu.

   1) Dare to ginkō e ikimasu ka. (Ali-san) ······
   2) Dare to Nihon e kimashita ka. (tomodachi) ······
   3) Dare to byōin e ikimashita ka. (Tanaka-san) ······
   4) Dare to Sentā e kaerimashita ka. (hitori de) ······

4. Rei : Itsu Kyōto e ikimasu ka. (ashita) ······Ashita ikimasu.

  1) Itsu Hiroshima e ikimasu ka. (raigetsu) ······

  2) Itsu Sentā e kimashita ka. (senshū) ······

  3) Itsu Nihon e kimashita ka. (6-gatsu tōka ni) ······

  4) Itsu kuni e kaerimasu ka. (rainen 3-gatsu ni) ······

5. Rei : Tanjōbi wa itsu desu ka. ······1-gatsu itsuka desu.

  1) Anata no tanjōbi wa itsu desu ka. ······ しヮ じゅうご にち です。

  2) Lee-san no tanjōbi wa itsu desu ka. ······はち月 ついたち です。

  3) Rao-san no tanjōbi wa itsu desu ka.······く月 はつか です。

  4) Sensei no tanjōbi wa itsu desu ka. ······じゅう いち月 にじゅうさん にちです

                    [どん月 むいかです]

Rei	1						
	S	M	T	W	T	F	S
		1	2	3	4	⑤	6
	7	8	9	10	11	12	13
	14	15	16	17	18	19	20
	21	22	23	24	25	26	27
	28	29	30	31			

1)	4						
	S	M	T	W	T	F	S
	1	2	3	4	5	6	7
	8	9	10	11	12	13	14
	⑮	16	17	18	19	20	21
	22	23	24	25	26	27	28
	29	30					

2)	8						
	S	M	T	W	T	F	S
			①	2	3	4	
	5	6	7	8	9	10	11
	12	13	14	15	16	17	18
	19	20	21	22	23	24	25
	26	27	28	29	30	31	

3)	9						
	S	M	T	W	T	F	S
							1
	2	3	4	5	6	7	8
	9	10	11	12	13	14	15
	16	17	18	19	⑳	21	22
	23	24	25	26	27	28	29
	30						

4)	11						
	S	M	T	W	T	F	S
					1	2	3
	4	5	6	7	8	9	10
	11	12	13	14	15	16	17
	18	19	20	21	22	㉓	24
	25	26	27	28	29	30	

たたしい ですか。

Renshū C

1. A : Kaisha wa dochira desu ka.

   B : <u>Tōkyō-denki</u> desu.
   ①
   A : Mainichi nan de ikimasu ka.

   B : <u>Densha</u> de ikimasu.
   ②

   1）　① Nagoya-jidōsha　② chikatetsu
   2）　① Yokohama-denki　② basu
   3）　① Ōsaka-kikai　② densha to basu

2. A : Nichi-yōbi doko e ikimashita ka.

   B : Hiroshima e ikimashita.

   A : Sō desu ka.　Hitori de ikimashita ka.

   B : Iie, <u>tomodachi</u> to ikimashita.

   1）　Ali-san
   2）　Katō-san
   3）　kaisha no hito

3. A : Itsu Tōkyō e ikimasu ka.

   B : <u>Ashita</u> ikimasu.
   ①
   A : Nan-ji ni ikimasu ka.

   B : <u>Asa 9-ji</u> ni ikimasu.
   ②

   1）　① konban　② 7-ji
   2）　① asatte　② gogo 1-ji
   3）　① ashita no asa　② 8-ji

Mondai

1. 1) _____
   2) _____
   3) _____
   4) _____
   5) _____

2.
Rei : Ali-san wa ⎰ ⓐ hitori de
                  ⎱ b. tomodachi to ⎰ (sūpā) e ikimasu.
                    c. Rao-san to

1) Narong-san wa ashita (Hiroshima) e ⎰ a. ikimasu.
                                         ⎱ b. kimasu.
                                           c. kaerimasu.

2) Ashita ⎰ a. densha
            ⎱ b. shinkansen ⎰ de (tokyo.) e ikimasu.
              c. hikōki ✓

3) Nichi-yōbi ⎰ a. hitori de
                ⎱ b. koibito to ✓ (Osaka) e ikimashita.
                  c. Lee-san to

4) ⎰ a. 7-gatsu
     ⎱ b. 8-gatsu ✓ (13)-nichi ni Nihon e kimashita.
       c. 9-gatsu

5) Rao-san wa (43)-sai desu.

    Tanjōbi wa ⎰ a. 4-gatsu tōka
                ⎱ b. 7-gatsu tōka ⎰ desu.
                  c. 10-gatsu yokka ✓

42

3. Rei : Kore wa [dare] (no) tokei desu ka.

······Watashi no tokei desu.

1) [いつ] Nihon e kimashita ka. ······9-gatsu 11-nichi ni kimashita.

2) [だれ] (と) Nihon e kimashita ka. ······Han-san to kimashita.

3) Nichi-yōbi [どこ] (へ) ikimasu ka. ······Depāto e ikimasu.

······Doko mo ikimasen.

4) Sumimasen. Tōkyō made [いくら] desu ka. ······560-en desu.

5) [なん] (で) Kyōto e ikimasu ka. ······Shinkansen de ikimasu.

6) [いつ] kuni e kaerimasu ka. ······Rainen 3-gatsu ni kaerimasu.

7) Kyō wa [なん月 がつ] [なん 日 にち] desu ka. ······12-gatsu 25-nichi desu.

4. 1) Hajimemashite. Watashi (wa) Indo (の) Rao desu.

Sengetsu 15-nichi (に) Nihon (へ) kimashita.

Tōkyō-denki (の) kenshūsei desu. Senmon (は) konpyūtā desu.

2) Kinō watashi wa Ali-san (と) Yokohama (へ) ikimashita.

Yokohama made basu (で) ikimashita. 6-ji (に) takushii

(で) Sentā (へ) kaerimashita.

Dai 6 ka

Bunkei

1. Watashi wa kōhii o nomimasu.
2. Watashi wa depāto de shatsu o kaimasu. *Polite Invitation, why don't we. / would you like...*
3. Issho ni gohan o tabemasen ka.
4. Robii de yasumimashō. *let's...*

Reibun

1. Anata wa tabako o suimasu ka.

   ···Iie, suimasen.

2. Maiasa nani o tabemasu ka.

   ···Pan to tamago o tabemasu.

3. Kesa nani o tabemashita ka. *Can you say this?*

   ···Nani mo tabemasendeshita. *Nani mo shimasendeshita = nothing else.*

4. Kinō no ban nani o shimashita ka.

   ···Nihon-go o benkyō-shimashita.   Sorekara tegami o kakimashita.

5. Doko de sono kutsu o kaimashita ka.

   ···Depāto de kaimashita.

6. Issho ni depāto e ikimasen ka.

   ···Ē, ikimashō.

Kaiwa

Eiga ni iku

Rao : Moshi moshi, Satō-san desu ka.　Rao desu.

Satō : Ā, Rao-san.　Konbanwa.

Rao : Ashita hima desu ka.

Satō : Ē.

Rao : Ja, issho ni Yokohama de eiga o mimasen ka.

Satō : Ii desu ne.　Doko de aimasu ka.

Rao : 3-ji ni Yokohama-eki de aimashō.

Satō : Wakarimashita.

Rao : Ja, mata ashita.

45

Renshū A

1. Watashi wa | ringo | o tabemasu.
   | sakana |
   | niku to yasai |
   Anata wa | nani | ·············· ka.

2. Watashi wa nani mo | tabe masen. |
   | nomi masen. |
   | kai masendeshita. |

3. Watashi wa | depāto | de kaban o kaimashita.
   | Ginza |
   | Ōsaka |
   Anata wa | doko | ···························· ka.

4. Issho ni | biiru o | nomi masen ka. |
   | gohan o | tabe masen ka. |
   | Kyōto e | iki masen ka. |

5. | owari masu | → | owari mashō |
benkyō-shi masu		benkyō-shi mashō
iki masu		iki mashō
tabe masu		tabe mashō

Renshū B

1. Rei : ······ terebi o mimasu

☞ 1) ······

2) ······

3) ······

4) ······

5) ······

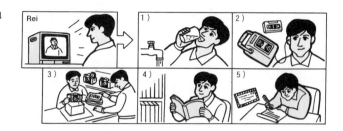

6

2. Rei : Tabako o suimasu ka. (hai) ······ Hai, suimasu.

1) O-sake o nomimasu ka. (iie) ······

2) Maiban terebi o mimasu ka. (hai) ······

3) Kesa shinbun o yomimashita ka. (iie) ······

4) Kinō no ban Nihon-go o benkyō-shimashita ka. (hai) ······

3. Rei : Nani o nomimasu ka. (jūsu) ······Jūsu o nomimasu.

1) Nani o kaimasu ka. (kutsu) ······

2) Nani o nomimasu ka. (kōcha) ······

3) Nani o tabemasu ka. (gohan to sakana) ······

4) Nani o jisshū-shimasu ka. (konpyūtā) ······

47

4. Rei : Doko de bangohan o tabemasu ka. (Ginza) ······Ginza de tabemasu.

1) Doko de eiga o mimasu ka. (Yokohama) ······

2) Doko de konpyūtā o jisshū-shimasu ka. (Tōkyō) ······

3) Doko de firumu o kaimashita ka. (uketsuke) ······

4) Doko de kono shashin o torimashita ka. (kōjō) ······

5. Rei : Konban nani o shimasu ka. ······Tomodachi to pinpon o shimasu.

☞ 1) Nichi-yōbi nani o shimasu ka. ······

2) Mainichi Sentā de nani o shimasu ka. ······

3) Kinō no ban nani o shimashita ka. ······

4) Ginza de nani o shimashita ka. ······

6. Rei : Konban nani o shimasu ka.

(terebi o mimasu,   Nihon-go o benkyō-shimasu)

······Terebi o mimasu.   Sorekara Nihon-go o benkyō-shimasu.

1) Ashita nani o shimasu ka.

(Nihon-go o benkyō-shimasu,   kōgi o kikimasu) ······

2) Kinō no ban nani o shimashita ka.

(hon o yomimasu,   tegami o kakimasu) ······

3) Nichi-yōbi nani o shimashita ka.

(Ginza de gohan o tabemasu,   eiga o mimasu) ······

4) Nihon de nani o shimasu ka.

(Nihon-go o benkyō-shimasu,   kōjō de jisshū-shimasu) ······

7. Rei : Issho ni Tōkyō e ikimasen ka. ······Ē, ikimashō.

1) Issho ni shashin o torimasen ka. ······

2) Issho ni ocha o nomimasen ka. ······

3) Issho ni hirugohan o tabemasen ka. ······

4) Issho ni pinpon o shimasen ka. ······

Renshū C

1. A : Kinō no ban nani o shimashita ka.
   B : 9-ji made terebi o mimashita.
   A : Sō desu ka. Sorekara nani o shimashita ka.
   B : <u>Nihon-go o benkyō-shi</u>mashita.

   1） tegami o kakimasu
   2） tēpu o kikimasu
   3） hon o yomimasu

2. A : Nichi-yōbi nani o shimasu ka.
   B : Eiga o mimasu.
   A : Doko de mimasu ka.
   B : <u>Ginza</u> de mimasu.

   1） Yokohama
   2） Nagoya
   3） Shinjuku

3. A : Konban issho ni <u>biiru o nomi</u>masen ka.
   B : Ē, ii desu ne.
   A : Ja, 7-ji ni robii de aimashō.

   1） eiga o mimasu
   2） gohan o tabemasu
   3） Tōkyō e ikimasu

Mondai

1. 1) _____
    2) _____
    3) _____
    4) _____
    5) _____

2.

1) Tanaka-san wa maiban (   ) o $\begin{cases} \text{a. kaimasu.} \\ \text{b. nomimasu.} \\ \text{c. nomimasen.} \end{cases}$

2) (   ) to (   ) o $\begin{cases} \text{a. tabemasu.} \\ \text{b. tabemasen.} \\ \text{c. tabemashita.} \end{cases}$

3) Nichi-yōbi no gogo (   ) to $\begin{cases} \text{a. Nihon-go o benkyō-shimashita.} \\ \text{b. tomodachi no uchi e ikimashita.} \\ \text{c. Ginza e ikimashita.} \end{cases}$

4) Kinō Shinjuku no (   ) de $\begin{cases} \text{a. shatsu o kaimashita.} \\ \text{b. kutsu o kaimashita.} \\ \text{c. nani mo kaimasendeshita.} \end{cases}$

5) Rao-san wa konban (   ) de $\begin{cases} \text{a. terebi o mimasu.} \\ \text{b. Amerika no eiga o mimasu.} \\ \text{c. Nihon no eiga o mimasu.} \end{cases}$

3.

Rei : tabako o suimasu

1) _____   5) _____

2) _____   6) _____

3) _____   7) _____

4) _____

4. Rei : [Nan] (de) ikimasu ka. ……Basu de ikimasu.

    1) Kinō [どこ] (へ) ikimashita ka. ……Depāto e ikimashita.

    2) Depāto de [何(なに)] (を) kaimashita ka.

        ……Nekutai o kaimashita.

        ……Nani mo kaimasendeshita.

    3) [どこ] (で) bangohan o tabemashita ka.

        ……Shinjuku de tabemashita.

    4) [何(なに)] (を) tabemashita ka.

        ……Sakana (と) yasai o tabemashita.

    5) A : Issho ni shashin (を) torimasen ka.

        B : Ii desu ne. [どこ] (で) torimasu ka.

        A : Niwa de torimashō.

    6) A : Ashita issho ni Ginza (へ) ikimasen ka.

        B : Ē, ii desu ne. [何じ] (に) ikimasu ka.

        A : 10-ji ni ikimashō.

6

51

5. 1) Watashi wa mainichi Sentā (de) Nihon-go (を) benkyō-shimasu.
Nihon-go (の) benkyō wa asa 9-ji (から) 12-ji (まで) desu.
Gogo wa kōgi desu. Kōgi wa 2-ji (から) desu. 5-ji (に)
owarimasu.

    2) Watashi wa kinō Satō-san (と) Yokohama (で) eiga o mimashita.
Eiga wa 6-ji (に) owarimashita. Sorekara issho ni bangohan
(を) tabemashita.

Fukushū A

1.

Rei : nemasu	nemasen	nemashita	nemasendeshita
ikimasu			
kaerimasu			
tabemasu			
nomimasu			
kaimasu			
kikimasu			
kakimasu			

2. Rei : Watashi (wa) Rao desu.

1) Watashi wa Indoneshia (の) Ali desu.

2) Yokohama-kikai (の) kenshūsei desu.

3) Senmon (は) kikai desu.

4) Lee-san wa Chūgoku-jin desu.　Han-san (も) Chūgoku-jin desu.

5) Kore (は) watashi (の) hon desu.

6) Kono hon wa Rao-san (の) desu.

7) Jimusho (は) doko desu ka.

8) Kono tokei (を) kudasai.

9) Watashi wa 8-ji (から) 4-ji (まで) hatarakimasu.

10) Maiban 12-ji (に) nemasu.

11) Nihon-go (の) benkyō wa 9-ji (から) 12-ji (まで) desu.

12) Rainen 3-gatsu (に) kuni (へ) kaerimasu.

13) Nichi-yōbi tomodachi (と) chikatetsu (で) Shinjuku (へ) ikimashita.

14) Shinjuku (で) kamera (と) tēpu-rekōdā (を) kaimashita.

15) Tomodachi wa nani (を) kaimasendeshita.

A

3. Rei : Ano hito wa [　dare　] desu ka. ……Lee-san desu.

1) [なんとし] desu ka. ……30-sai desu.

2) Kore wa [　何　] desu ka. ……Haizara desu.

3) Sore wa [だれ] no kaban desu ka.
……Rao-san no kaban desu.

4) Kono bōrupen wa [だれ] no desu ka. ……Watashi no desu.

5) Otearai wa [どこ] desu ka. ……Asoko desu.

6) Uketsuke wa [どちら] desu ka. ……Sochira desu.

7) Kaisha wa [どちら] desu ka. ……Ōsaka-Kikai desu.

8) Rao-san no kuni wa [どこ] desu ka. ……Indo desu.

9) Sore wa [どこ] no tokei desu ka. ……Nihon no tokei desu.

10) NTC wa [何] no kaisha desu ka.
……Konpyūtā no kaisha desu.

11) Kono kamera wa [いくら] desu ka. ……20,000-en desu.

12) Ima [何じ] desu ka. ……9-ji 15-fun desu.

13) Maiasa [何じ] ni okimasu ka. ……7-ji ni okimasu.

14) Kōgi wa [何じ] kara [何じ] made desu ka.
……2-ji kara 5-ji made desu.

15) Kyō wa [何よう日] desu ka. ……Ka-yōbi desu.

16) Ashita [どこ] e ikimasu ka. ……Kyōto e ikimasu.

17) [何(なに)] de Kyōto e ikimasu ka. ……Densha de ikimasu.

18) [だれ] to Kyōto e ikimasu ka. ……Tomodachi to ikimasu.

19) Tanjōbi wa [いつ] desu ka. ……8-gatsu tōka desu.

20) Kyō wa [何月][何日] desu ka.
……4-gatsu 15-nichi desu.

21) Kesa [何(なに)] o tabemashita ka. ……Pan o tabemashita.

22) Nichi-yōbi [何(なに)] o shimashita ka.
……Ginza de eiga o mimashita.

23) [どこ] de jisshū-shimasu ka.
……Tōkyō de jisshū-shimasu.

Dai 7 ka

Bunkei

1. Watashi wa hashi de gohan o tabemasu.

2. Watashi wa Lee-san ni tokei o agemasu.

3. Watashi wa Tanaka-san ni jisho o moraimashita.
   (kara)

   to

   from.

Reibun

1. Nan de rajio o shūri-shimasu ka.

   ···Doraibā de shūri-shimasu.

2. Nihon-go de repōto o kakimasu ka.

   ···Iie, Eigo de kakimasu.

3. Dare ni tegami o kakimashita ka.

   ···Kazoku ni kakimashita.

4. Dare ni Nihon-go o naraimashita ka.

   ···Kaisha no hito ni naraimashita.

5. Mō hirugohan o tabemashita ka.

   ···Hai, mō tabemashita.

6. Mō kaisha ni repōto o kakimashita ka.

   ···Iie, mada desu.　Korekara kakimasu.

Kaiwa

Purezento

Ali : Lee-san, tanjōbi omedetō gozaimasu.

     Kore wa purezento desu. Dōzo.

Lee : Wā, nan desu ka.

Ali : Indoneshia no shatsu desu.

Lee : Dōmo arigatō gozaimasu.

Ali : Dō itashimashite.

Tanaka: Ii shatsu desu ne.

Lee : Kore desu ka.

     Tanjōbi ni Ali-san ni moraimashita.

Renshū A

1. Watashi wa   hashi   de gohan o tabemasu.
                   supūn
                   fōku to naifu
   Anata wa   nan   .... ka.

2. Watashi wa   Nihon-go   de repōto o kakimasu.
                   Eigo
                   Chūgoku-go

3. Watashi wa   tomodachi   ni tegami o kakimasu.
                   kanai
                   koibito
   Anata wa   dare   .... ka.

4. Watashi wa   Satō-san   ni Nihon-go o naraimashita.
                   Suzuki-sensei
                   kaisha no hito
   Anata wa   dare   .... ka.

5. Mō   hirugohan o   tabe mashita.
        kono hon o   yomi mashita.
        kazoku ni tegami o   kaki mashita.

Renshū B

1. Rei :　Nan de gohan o tabemasu ka. ······Hashi de tabemasu.
   1)　Nan de tegami o kakimasu ka. ······
   2)　Nan de niku o kirimasu ka. ······
   3)　Nan de jidōsha o shūri-shimasu ka. ······
   4)　Nan de kami o kirimasu ka. ······

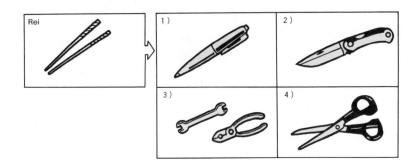

2. Rei :　Dare ni tegami o kakimasu ka. (otōto) ······Otōto ni kakimasu.
   1)　Dare ni denwa o kakemasu ka. (shujin) ······
   2)　Dare ni jisho o kashimashita ka. (Lee-san) ······
   3)　Dare ni tegami o kakimashita ka. (kodomo) ······
   4)　Suzuki-sensei wa dare ni Nihon-go o oshiemasu ka. (kenshūsei) ······

3. Rei :　Dare ni sono hon o moraimashita ka. (sensei)
   　　　　······Sensei ni moraimashita.
   1)　Dare ni Nihon-go o naraimashita ka. (Suzuki-sensei) ······
   2)　Dare ni sono purezento o moraimashita ka. (Kimura-san) ······
   3)　Dare ni sono jisho o karimashita ka. (Tanaka-san) ······
   4)　Dare ni Eigo o naraimashita ka. (kaisha no hito) ······

4. Rei : Okāsan ni nani o agemasu ka. ······Okane o agemasu.

☞ 1) Koibito ni nani o moraimashita ka. ······

2) Okusan ni nani o agemasu ka. ······

3) Otōsan ni nani o agemasu ka. ······

4) Kaisha no hito ni nani o moraimashita ka. ······

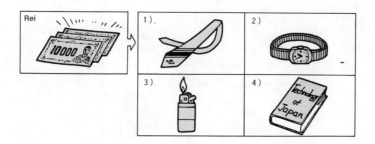

5. Rei 1 : Mō asagohan o tabemashita ka. (hai) ······Hai, mō tabemashita.

Rei 2 : Mō hirugohan o tabemashita ka. (iie) ······Iie, mada desu.

1) Mō tēpu o kikimashita ka. (hai) ······

2) Mō Nihon no eiga o mimashita ka. (iie) ······

3) Mō kaisha ni repōto o kakimashita ka. (iie) ······

4) Mō kazoku ni tegami o kakimashita ka. (hai) ······

Renshū C

1. A : Sore wa nan desu ka.

   B : Kore desu ka. <u>Hon</u> desu.
   ①
   <u>Rao-san</u> ni agemasu.
   ②

   1) ① tokei   ② kaisha no hito
   2) ① tēpu   ② tomodachi
   3) ① shashin ② sensei

2. A : Kuni de Nihon-go o naraimashita ka.

   B : Hai, naraimashita.

   A : Sensei wa Nihon-jin desu ka.

   B : Iie, <u>Tai-jin</u> no sensei ni naraimashita.

   1) Chūgoku-jin
   2) Indoneshia-jin
   3) Indo-jin

3. A : Mō <u>repōto</u> o <u>kakimashita</u> ka.

   B : Iie, mada desu.

      Korekara <u>kakimasu</u>.

   1) bangohan o tabemasu
   2) tēpu o kikimasu
   3) kaisha ni denwa o kakemasu

Mondai

1. 1) _____

    2) _____

    3) _____

    4) _____

    5) _____

2.

1) Korekara issho ni (ごはん) o
{ a. tabemasu.
  b. tabemasen.
  c. tabemashita. }

2) (えき) de kaisha ni
{ a. tegami o kakimashita.
  b. repōto o kakimashita.
  c. denwa o kakemashita. }

3) (はは) to tomodachi ni
{ a. tegami o kakimasu.
  b. denwa o kakemashita.
  c. tegami o kakimashita. }

4) Lee-san wa tanjōbi ni (とけい) o
{ a. kashimashita.
  b. agemashita.
  c. moraimashita. }

5) Lee-san wa Chūgoku de Nihon-go o
{ a. moraimashita.
  b. naraimashita.
  c. oshiemashita. }

Sensei wa (日本人) desu.

3.

  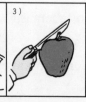

Rei : Lee-san ni okane o kashimasu.

1) Tomodachi ni _____

2) Koibito ni _____

3) Naifu de _____

4) Nihon-go de _____

5) Supana to doraibā de _____

4. Rei : [Nani] (o) nomimasu ka. ······Jūsu o nomimasu.

1) Nihon-jin wa [何] (で) gohan o tabemasu ka.

······Hashi de tabemasu.

2) [どこ] (で) Nihon-go o naraimashita ka.

······Kenshū Sentā de naraimashita.

3) [だれ] (に) Nihon-go o naraimashita ka.

······Suzuki-sensei ni naraimashita.

4) Okusan no tanjōbi ni [何] (を) agemashita ka.

······Tokei o agemashita.

5) Tanjōbi ni [何] (を) moraimashita ka.

······Bōrupen o moraimashita.

6) [だれ] (に) sono hon o karimashita ka.

······Tanaka-san ni karimashita.

5. Rei : Mō repōto o kakimashita ka. ······Hai, mō kakimashita.

1) Mō kono shinbun o yomimashita ka. ······Hai, そう よみました Dōzo.

2) Mō bangohan o tabemashita ka.

······Iie, まだ です . Korekara tabemasu.

3) Mō Kyōto e ikimashita ka. ······Iie, まだ です . Ashita ikimasu.

4) Mō kaisha ni denwa o kakemashita ka.

······ Iie, まだ です . Korekara kakemasu.

5) Tanaka-san wa mō uchi e kaerimashita ka. ······Hai, そう かえりました

6. 1) Ashita wa Lee-san (no) tanjōbi desu. Kinō watashi wa depāto

(で) nekutai (を) kaimashita. Ashita Lee-san (に) agemasu.

2) Kyō wa watashi (の) tanjōbi desu. Watashi wa Satō-san (から) (に)

nekutai (を) moraimashita.

おおい = a lot of (countable & unc)

あまり = not so

あんまり) = conv. Japanese

Bunkei

1. Rao-san wa shinsetsu desu. な

2. Tōkyō wa ōkii desu.

3. Rao-san wa shinsetsuna hito desu.

4. Tōkyō wa ōkii machi desu.

Reibun

1. Sentā wa shizuka desu ka.

   ···Hai, shizuka desu.   な

   ···Iie, shizuka dewa arimasen.

2. Tai wa ima atsui desu ka.
   とても
   ···Hai, taihen atsui desu.

   ···Iie, amari atsukunai desu.
        not so   neg.

3. Sono jisho wa ii desu ka.

   ···Iie, amari yokunai desu.

4. Nihon no tabemono wa dō desu ka.
                              but
   ···Oishii desu ga, takai desu.

5. Kimura-san wa donna hito desu ka.

   ···Kireina hito desu.   Soshite taihen shinsetsu desu.

                       which. More than 3.   どっち =which out
                                                       of 2.
6. Rao-san no kaban wa dore desu ka.

   ···Ano kuroi kaban desu.

いや（な）= nasty.

Kaiwa

Sentā hōmon

としぶり

Katō : Yā, Rao-san, shibaraku desu ne.

O-genki desu ka.

Rao : Hai, genki desu.

Dōzo kochira e.

何かのみものは ...... = anything to drink?

Rao : Kōhii wa ikaga desu ka.

Katō : A, dōmo.

Itadakimasu.

Oishii kōhii desu ne.

How is it?
(& also How about)

Nihon-go no benkyō wa dō desu ka.

Rao : Sō desu ne. Muzukashii desu ga, omoshiroi desu.

but

Renshū A

1. Kimura-san wa   kirei   desu.   な + でわ ありません。
                 genki   じゃ なし。
                 shinsetsu

2. Kono kaban wa   chiisa i   desu.   い + くなし です。
                 taka i   くなし。
                 atarashi i

3.   kirei desu   kirei dewa arimasen
     genki desu   ⟶   genki dewa arimasen
     shizuka desu   shizuka dewa arimasen

4.   waru i desu   waru kunai desu
     omoshiro i desu   ⟶   omoshiro kunai desu
          i i desu   yo kunai desu

5. Kimura-san wa   kirei na   hito desu.
                 genki na
                 shinsetsu na

6. Kore wa   i i   kaban desu.
           taka i
           atarashi i

8

Renshū B

1. Rei : ·····Kono shatsu wa takai desu.
   ☞ 1) ······
   2) ······
   3) ······
   4) ······

(handwritten: いけん)

(handwritten: ば"s = rose .)

2. Rei 1 : ano hito wa shinsetsu desu
   ······Ano hito wa shinsetsu dewa arimasen.
   Rei 2 : kyō wa atsui desu
   ······Kyō wa atsukunai desu.
   1) kono hon wa omoshiroi desu ······
   2) watashi no heya wa kirei desu ······
   3) kono jisho wa ii desu ······
   4) kono machi wa shizuka desu ······

3. Rei 1 : Nihon no kamera wa yasui desu ka. (hai) ·····Hai, yasui desu. *(い)*
   Rei 2 : Kyō wa samui desu ka. (iie) ·····Iie, samukunai desu. *(い)*
   1) Shukudai wa muzukashii desu ka. (iie) ······ *(い)*
   2) Nara wa shizuka desu ka. (hai) ······ *(だ)*
   3) Nihon no tabemono wa takai desu ka. (hai) ······ *(い)*
   4) Lee-san wa genki desu ka. (iie) ······ *(だ)*

4. Rei 1 : Shinjuku wa nigiyaka desu ka. (hai, taihen) *(handwritten: lively.)*
   ······Hai, taihen nigiyaka desu.
   Rei 2 : Nihon no tabemono wa oishii desu ka. (iie, amari)
   ······Iie, amari oishikunai desu.
   (handwritten: observing/sightseeing)
   1) Kengaku wa omoshiroi desu ka. (hai, taihen) ······ *(い)*
   2) Anata no kuni wa ima atsui desu ka. (iie, amari) ······ *(い)*
   3) Kimura-san wa shinsetsu desu ka. (hai, taihen) ······ *(だ)*
   4) Kono tēpu-rekōdā wa ii desu ka. (iie, amari) ······ *(い)*

5. Rei : Nihon no tabemono wa dō desu ka. (oishii) ······Oishii desu.

   1) Nihon-go no benkyō wa dō desu ka. (omoshiroi) ······

   2) Shiken wa dō desu ka. (yasashii) ······

   3) Tōkyō wa dō desu ka. (nigiyaka) ······

   4) Nihon no kamera wa dō desu ka. (taihen ii) ······

8

6. Rei 1 : kore wa hana desu (kirei) ······Kore wa kireina hana desu.

   Rei 2 : kore wa kamera desu (ii) ······Kore wa ii kamera desu.

   1) kore wa gyūnyū desu (tsumetai) ······ い

   2) Suzuki-san wa sensei desu (shinsetsu) ······ な

   3) kore wa zasshi desu (atarashii) ······い

   4) sakura wa hana desu (yūmei) ······ な

66

7. Rei : Kyōto wa shizukana machi desu ka. (iie) ? ALWAYS? でわ ありません.

   ······Iie, shizukana machi dewa arimasen.

   1) Mirion wa ōkii kaisha desu ka. (iie) ······ミリオンは おおきじ づいじゃ であありません。

   2) Rao-san wa shinsetsuna hito desu ka. (hai) ······

   3) Sore wa omoshiroi hon desu ka. (iie) ······

   4) Sakura wa kireina hana desu ka. (hai) ······

8. Rei : Chūgoku wa donna kuni desu ka. (ōkii) ······Ōkii kuni desu.

   1) Fujisan wa donna yama desu ka. (takai) ······ い

   2) Rao-san wa donna hito desu ka. (hansamu) ······ な

   3) Nara wa donna machi desu ka. (furui) ······ い

   4) Ginza wa donna tokoro desu ka. (taihen nigiyaka) ······ な

   place

Renshū C

1. A : O-genki desu ka.

   B : Hai, genki desu.

   A : <u>Nihon-go no benkyō</u> wa dō desu ka.
   　　　①

   B : Sō desu ne. <u>Muzukashii desu ga, omoshiroi desu.</u>
   　　　　　　　　　　　②

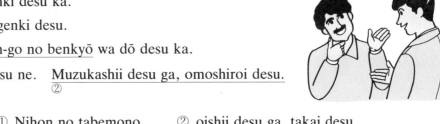

   1)　① Nihon no tabemono　　② oishii desu ga, takai desu

   2)　① kōgi　　② omoshiroi desu ga, muzukashii desu

   3)　① Nihon　　② kirei desu ga, samui desu

   8

2. A : Kinō Tanaka-san no <u>koibito</u> ni aimashita.
   　　　　　　　　　　　　①

   B : Sō desu ka.　Donna hito desu ka.

   A : <u>Kireina</u> hito desu.　Soshite taihen ii hito desu.
   　　　②

   1)　① otōsan　　② genki desu な

   2)　① okāsan　　② omoshiroi desu い

   3)　① oniisan　　② hansamu desu な

   67

3. A : Are wa ikura desu ka.

   B : Dore desu ka.

   A : Ano <u>akai kaban</u> desu.
   　　　①

   B : Are wa <u>8,500-en</u> desu.
   　　　　　②

   1)　① kuroi kutsu　　② 10,000-en

   2)　① shiroi shatsu　　② 3,000-en

   3)　① aoi nekutai　　② 5,000-en

Mondai

8

1. 1) _____
   [cassette] 2) _____
   3) _____
   4) _____
   5) _____

2.
   [cassette] 1) Ashita no (   ) wa $\begin{cases} \text{a. muzukashii desu.} \\ \text{b. taihen yasashii desu.} \\ \text{c. taihen yasui desu.} \end{cases}$

   2) Nihon no (   ) wa $\begin{cases} \text{a. atsui desu.} \\ \text{b. tsumetai desu.} \\ \text{c. oishii desu.} \end{cases}$

   3) Shinjuku wa (   ) desu ga, $\begin{cases} \text{a. nigiyakana} \\ \text{b. shizukana} \\ \text{c. kireina} \end{cases}$ machi desu.

   4) Satō-san wa $\begin{cases} \text{a. genkina} \\ \text{b. yūmeina} \\ \text{c. kireina} \end{cases}$ hito desu.

   Soshite taihen (   ) desu.

   5) Ano $\begin{cases} \text{a. shiroi} \\ \text{b. chiisai} \\ \text{c. takai} \end{cases}$ kaban wa (   )-en desu.

3. Rei : ōkii …… (chiisai   )
   1） samui …… (あつい)
   2） muzukashii …… (やさしい)
   3） ii …… (わるい)
   4） yasui …… (たかい)
   5） atarashii …… (ふるい)
   6） tsumetai …… (あつい)
   7） hikui …… (たかい)

4. Rei : Anata no kuni wa ima atsui desu ka. ……Iie, amari atsukunai desu.
   1） Anata no kuni no jidōsha wa yasui desu ka.
   ……Iie, あまり やすくない です. Taihen takai desu.
   2） Sono kamera wa ii desu ka. ……Iie, amari よくない です
   3） Shiken wa muzukashii desu ka. ……Iie, あまり むずかしく ない です Yasashii desu.
   4） Lee-san wa genki desu ka. ……Iie, あまり げんき でわ ありません。
   5） Sono kutsu wa ōkii desu ka. ……Iie, あまり おおくない です。
   6） Tōkyō wa shizuka desu ka.
   ……Iie, あまり しずか でわ ありません. Taihen nigiyaka desu.

69

5. Rei : Shinjuku wa (nigiyaka desu … nigiyakana) machi desu.
   Senshū watashi wa tomodachi to Nara e ikimashita. Nara wa taihen
   (furui desu … ふるい) machi desu. Soshite (shizuka desu … しずかな)
   machi desu. Watashi-tachi wa (yūmei desu … ゆうめいな) *Wakakusa-yama e
   ikimashita. Wakakusa-yama wa amari (takai desu …   ) nai desu ga,
   kirei desu. Watashi-tachi wa sakura o mimashita. Sakura wa taihen
   (kirei desu … きれいな) hana desu.

*Wakakusa-yama—yama no namae

Dai 9 ka

Bunkei

1. Watashi wa ringo ga suki desu.
2. Watashi wa kamera ga arimasu.
3. Watashi wa onaka ga itai desu kara, byōin e ikimasu.

Reibun

1. Anata wa biiru ga suki desu ka.

   ···Iie, suki dewa arimasen.

2. Donna supōtsu ga suki desu ka.

   ···Tenisu ga suki desu.

3. Ali-san wa uta ga jōzu desu ka.

   ···Hai, taihen jōzu desu.

4. Anata wa ima okane ga arimasu ka.

   ···Hai, sukoshi arimasu.

5. Anata wa kanji ga wakarimasu ka.

   ···Iie, zenzen wakarimasen.

6. Konban doko e ikimasu ka.

   ···Shukudai ga takusan arimasu kara, doko mo ikimasen.

7. Dōshite kaisha o yasumimashita ka.

   ···Netsu ga arimashita kara.

Kaiwa

Byōki

Rao   : Tanaka-san.

Tanaka : Hai, nan desu ka.

Rao   : Sumimasen ga, kusuri o kudasai.

Tanaka : Dō shimashita ka.

Rao   : Kaze o hikimashita.

Tanaka : Netsu ga arimasu ka.

Rao   : Ē, sukoshi arimasu.

Tanaka : Ja, byōin e ikimashō.

Rao   : Onegai-shimasu.

Renshū A

1. Watashi wa   ringo   ga suki desu.
                  eiga
                  ongaku

2. Mario-san wa   uta   ga jōzu desu.
                  pinpon
                  gitā

3. Watashi wa   kamera   ga arimasu.
                  jidōsha
                  tēpu-rekōdā

4. Watashi wa   kanji   ga wakarimasu.
                  hiragana
                  Nihon-go

5.   Okane ga arimasen   kara, doko mo ikimasen.
     Atama ga itai desu
     Netsu ga arimasu

9

Renshū B

1. Rei : Anata wa butaniku ga suki desu ka. (iie) ······Iie, suki dewa arimasen.
   1) Ali-san wa toriniku ga suki desu ka. (hai) ······
   2) Anata wa biiru ga suki desu ka. (iie) ······
   3) Kimura-san wa eiga ga suki desu ka. (hai, taihen) ······
   4) Rao-san wa pinpon ga suki desu ka. (iie, amari) ······

2. Rei : Donna supōtsu ga suki desu ka. (sakkā) ······Sakkā ga suki desu.
   1) Donna kudamono ga suki desu ka. (mikan)······
   2) Donna ryōri ga suki desu ka. (Tai-ryōri) ······
   3) Donna nomimono ga suki desu ka. (jūsu) ······
   4) Donna supōtsu ga suki desu ka. (tenisu) ······

3. Rei : Ali-san wa gitā ga jōzu desu ka. (hai) ······Hai, jōzu desu.
   1) Mario-san wa uta ga jōzu desu ka. (hai) ······
   2) Anata wa dansu ga jōzu desu ka. (iie) ······
   3) Lee-san wa Nihon-go ga jōzu desu ka. (hai, taihen) ······
   4) Anata wa tenisu ga jōzu desu ka. (iie, amari) ······

4. Rei : Anata wa kamera ga arimasu ka. (hai) ······Hai, arimasu.
   1) Suzuki-san wa jidōsha ga arimasu ka. (iie) ······
   2) Anata wa jisho ga arimasu ka. (iie) ······
   3) Kyō shukudai ga arimasu ka. (hai, sukoshi) ······
   4) Ano hito wa okane ga arimasu ka. (hai, takusan) ······

5. Rei : Rōmaji ga wakarimasu ka. (hai, yoku) ······Hai, yoku wakarimasu.
   1)   Nihon-go ga wakarimasu ka. (hai, sukoshi) ······
   2)   Eigo ga wakarimasu ka. (iie, amari) ······
   3)   Kanji ga wakarimasu ka. (iie, zenzen) ······
   4)   Kōgi ga wakarimasu ka. (hai, yoku) ······

6. Rei : kōhii ga suki desu, maiasa nomimasu
           ······Kōhii ga suki desu kara, maiasa nomimasu.
   1)   jikan ga arimasen, amari terebi o mimasen ······
   2)   kuni de benkyō-shimashita, Nihon-go ga sukoshi wakarimasu ······
   3)   kaze o hikimashita, byōin e ikimasu ······
   4)   atama ga itai desu, heya de nemasu ······

7. Rei : Dōshite depāto de kaimasen ka. (takai desu) ······Takai desu kara.
   1)   Dōshite biiru o nomimasen ka. (suki dewa arimasen) ······
   2)   Dōshite terebi o mimasen ka. (omoshirokunai desu) ······
   3)   Dōshite gohan o tabemasen ka. (onaka ga itai desu) ······
   4)   Dōshite kaisha o yasumimashita ka. (netsu ga arimashita) ······

9

Renshū C

1. A : <u>Eiga</u> ga suki desu ka.
   　　　①

   B : Ē, suki desu.

   A : Ja, nichi-yōbi issho ni <u>Yokohama de mi</u>masen ka.
   　　　　　　　　　　　　　　　　②

   B : Ii desu ne.

   1) ① o-sake　　② Shinjuku de nomimasu

   2) ① tenisu　　② Sentā de shimasu

   3) ① ongaku　　② uchi de kikimasu

2. A : Maiban terebi o mimasu ka.

   B : Iie, amari mimasen.

   　　<u>Jikan ga arimasen</u> kara.

   1) omoshirokunai desu

   2) shukudai ga takusan arimasu

   3) Nihon-go ga wakarimasen

3. A : Dō shimashita ka.

   B : <u>Onaka ga itai desu.</u>

   A : Ja, byōin e ikimashō.

   B : Ē, onegai-shimasu.

   1) atama ga itai desu

   2) netsu ga arimasu

   3) kaze o hikimashita

Mondai

1. 1) _____
    2) _____
    3) _____
    4) _____
    5) _____

2. 1) Kimura-san wa { a. kodomo / b. ringo / c. mikan } ga (   ) desu.

    2) Ali-san wa { a. gitā ga jōzu desu. / b. dansu ga jōzu desu. / c. gitā ga heta desu. } (   ) ni naraimashita.

    3) Lee-san wa katakana ga { a. daitai / b. sukoshi / c. zenzen } (   ).

    4) { a. Kanji ga wakarimasen / b. Okane ga arimasen / c. Jikan ga arimasen } kara, maiasa (   ) o yomimasen.

    5) Kinō (   ) kara, { a. kaisha o yasumimashita. / b. kaisha e ikimashita. / c. byōin e ikimashita. }

3. Rei : Gohan (o) tabemasu.
    1) Ali-san wa uta (が) jōzu desu.
    2) Donna supōtsu (が) suki desu ka.
    3) Kanji (が) zenzen wakarimasen.
    4) Watashi wa sakana (が) kirai desu kara, sakana (を) tabemasen.
    5) Jikan (が) arimasen kara, takushii de ikimashō.

4. Rei : kono heya wa kirei desu (amari)

        ······Kono heya wa amari kirei dewa arimasen.

1) watashi wa toriniku ga suki desu (amari) ······

2) kanai wa ryōri ga jōzu desu (amari) ······

3) watashi wa hiragana ga wakarimasu (zenzen) ······

4) kono mikan wa oishii desu (amari) ······

5) kono tokei wa ii desu (amari) ······

6) Kim-san wa tenisu ga jōzu desu (taihen) ······

7) Lee-san wa o-sake o nomimasu (takusan) ······

5. Rei : Depāto wa takai desu kara, (e)   a. nani mo kaimasen.

1) O-sake ga suki desu kara, (c)   b. tsumetai jūsu o nomimasu.

2) Onaka ga itai desu kara, (f.)   c. maiban nomimasu.

3) Okane ga arimasen kara, (a.)   d. Sentā de naraimasu.

4) Nihon-go ga wakarimasen kara, (d.)   e. sūpā de kaimasu.

5) Atsui desu kara, (b.)   f. kusuri o nomimasu.

6. Rei : Dōshite dansu o shimasen ka.

        ······Dansu ga heta desu kara.

1) Dōshite terebi o mimasen ka.

    ······ テレビ が きらい です から。

2) Dōshite byōin e ikimasu ka.

    ······ おなが が いたい です から。

3) Dōshite biiru o nomimasen ka.

    ······ きのう ビール を たくさん のみました から。

4) Dōshite depāto de kamera o kaimasen ka.

    ······ お金 が ありません から

5) Dōshite Nihon-go o benkyō-shimasu ka.

    ······ よく はなしたい です から。

Dai 10 ka

Bunkei

1. Jimusho ni Tanaka-san ga imasu.

2. Robii ni terebi ga arimasu.

3. Rao-san wa heya ni imasu.

4. Hon wa tsukue no ue ni arimasu.

Reibun

1. Robii ni dare ga imasu ka.

   ···Lee-san ga imasu.

2. Niwa ni dare ga imasu ka.

   ···Dare mo imasen.

3. Tsukue no ue ni nani ga arimasu ka.

   ···Kaban ga arimasu.

4. Heya ni nani ga arimasu ka.

   ···Iroirona mono ga arimasu.   Beddo ya tsukue ya isu ga arimasu.

5. Tanaka-san wa ima doko ni imasu ka.

   ···Shokudō ni imasu.

6. Hon-ya wa doko ni arimasu ka.

   ···Eki no chikaku desu.   Ginkō to sūpā no aida ni arimasu.

Kaiwa

Michi o kiku

Rao   : Anō, chikaku ni yūbinkyoku ga arimasu ka.

Kimura : Ē, arimasu yo.   Eki no mae desu.

Rao   : Eki no mae?

Kimura : Wakarimasen ka.   Ja, ima chizu o kakimasu.

            Eki wa koko desu.

Rao   : Hai.

Kimura : Eki no mae ni depāto ga arimasu.

            Yūbinkyoku wa kono tonari desu.

Rao   : Arigatō.   Ja, itte mairimasu.

Kimura : Itte irasshai.

Renshū A

1. Kyōshitsu ni   Rao-san   ga imasu.
                  sensei
                  kenshūsei
                  dare   ·············· ka.

2. Asoko ni   kaban   ga arimasu.
              tokei
              terebi
              nani   ················ ka.

3. Sūpā no   mae   ni resutoran ga arimasu.
             tonari
             hidari

4. Tanaka-san wa   jimusho   ni imasu.
                   niwa
                   erebētā no mae
                   doko   ·············· ka.

5. Hon-ya wa   asoko   ni arimasu.
               eki no chikaku
               ginkō no tonari
               doko   ················ ka.

Renshū B

1. Rei 1 :   asoko, otoko no hito ······Asoko ni otoko no hito ga imasu.

   Rei 2 :   robii, terebi ······Robii ni terebi ga arimasu.

   1) soko, haizara ······

   2) robii, kaisha no hito ······

   3) uketsuke, denwa ······

   4) kōen, onna no ko ······

   5) robii, shinbun ya zasshi ······

2. Rei :   Tsukue no ue ni nani ga arimasu ka. ······Pasupōto ga arimasu.

   1) Terebi no ue ni nani ga arimasu ka. ······

   2) Uchi no naka ni dare ga imasu ka. ······

   3) Han-san no ushiro ni nani ga arimasu ka. ······

   4) Niwa ni dare ga imasu ka. ······

   5) Hako no naka ni nani ga arimasu ka. ······

3. Rei : Tanaka-san wa doko ni imasu ka. (jimusho)
   ······Jimusho ni imasu.

   1） Narong-san wa doko ni imasu ka. (heya) ······
   2） Hasami wa doko ni arimasu ka. (tsukue no naka) ······
   3） Sūpā wa doko ni arimasu ka. (eki no mae) ······
   4） Kaisha no hito wa doko ni imasu ka. (robii) ······
   5） Serotēpu wa doko ni arimasu ka. (sono hako no naka) ······

4. Rei : Tanaka-san wa doko ni imasu ka. ······Sentā no mae ni imasu.

   1） Sūpā wa doko ni arimasu ka. ······
   2） Sentā no chikaku ni gakkō ga arimasu ka. ······
   3） Sentā no mae ni nani ga arimasu ka. ······
   4） Kōen ni kodomo ga imasu ka. ······
   5） Yūbinkyoku wa doko ni arimasu ka. ······

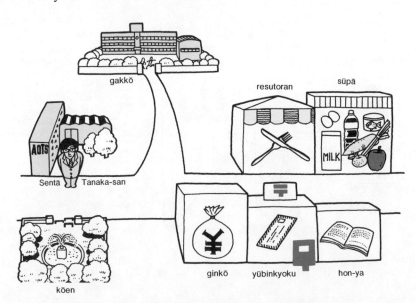

Renshū C

1. A : Asoko ni <u>shiroi</u> biru ga arimasu ne.
          ①
    B : Ē.
    A : Are wa nan desu ka.
    B : <u>Byōin</u> desu.
          ②

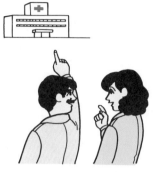

    1)   ① ōkii   ② yūbinkyoku
    2)   ① takai   ② depāto
    3)   ① furui   ② taishikan

2. A : Tanaka-san wa jimusho ni imasu ka.
    B : Iie, imasen.
        <u>Kōjō</u> e ikimashita.

    1)   mō uchi e kaerimashita
    2)   10-ji ni kimasu
    3)   taishikan e ikimashita

3. A : <u>Hasami</u> wa doko desu ka.
          ①
    B : Soko ni arimasu yo.
    A : Doko desu ka.
    B : Soko desu.   Sono <u>kami no shita</u> desu.
                          ②

    1)   ① serotēpu   ② hako no naka
    2)   ① keshigomu   ② nōto no aida
    3)   ① hotchikisu   ② hon no shita

Mondai

1.
1) _____
2) _____
3) _____
4) _____
5) _____

2.
1)
$$\left\{ \begin{array}{l} \text{a. Ginkō} \\ \text{b. Byōin} \\ \text{c. Yūbinkyoku} \end{array} \right\}$$ wa (   ) biru desu.

2) Denwa wa (   ) no $$\left\{ \begin{array}{l} \text{a. mae} \\ \text{b. migi} \\ \text{c. hidari} \end{array} \right\}$$ desu.

3) Suzuki-san wa $$\left\{ \begin{array}{l} \text{a. ima uketsuke ni imasu.} \\ \text{b. mō uchi e kaerimashita.} \\ \text{c. Sentā e ikimashita.} \end{array} \right\}$$

     Suzuki-san no uchi wa Sentā no (   ) ni arimasu.

4) (   ) wa $$\left\{ \begin{array}{l} \text{a. tsukue no ue} \\ \text{b. tsukue no naka} \\ \text{c. hako no naka} \end{array} \right\}$$ ni arimasu.

5) Posuto wa (   ) no $$\left\{ \begin{array}{l} \text{a. chikaku} \\ \text{b. mae} \\ \text{c. tonari} \end{array} \right\}$$ desu.

3. Rei : Asoko ni posuto ga (arimasu).
1) Asoko ni takai biru ga (あります。).
2) Heya ni beddo ya tsukue ya isu ga (あります。).
3) Rao-san wa robii ni (います).
4) Kamera-ya wa eki no chikaku ni (あります。).
5) Niwa ni dare ga (います) ka. ……Dare mo (いません。).
6) Hako no naka ni nani ga (あります。) ka. ……Nani mo (ありません。).

4.

Watashi no kaisha (wa) eki no chikaku

(に) arimasu. Kaisha wa yūbinkyoku

(と) ginkō (の) aida ni arimasu.　Eki

no mae (に) depāto (が) arimasu.

Depāto (の) tonari (に) resutoran ga

arimasu.　Kono resutoran (で) mainichi

hirugohan (を) tabemasu.　Kaisha no

chikaku ni hana-ya (や) byōin (や) kōen

ga arimasu.

5.

Watashi wa Kankoku no Kim desu.　NTC no kenshūsei desu.

Watashi no heya wa 424 desu.　4-kai ni arimasu.　Chiisai desu ga, kirei desu.

Sentā ni shokudō ga arimasu.　Iroirona ryōri ga arimasu.　Kankoku-ryōri

mo arimasu.　Watashi wa mainichi Sentā no shokudō de gohan o tabemasu.

Taihen oishii desu.

Sentā kara eki made aruite 10-pun desu.　Eki no chikaku ni depāto ya

ōkii sūpā ga arimasu.　Taihen nigiyaka desu.

Rei :　Watashi no kuni wa Kankoku desu.　　　(○)

　　　　Watashi no kuni wa Chūgoku desu.　　　(×)

1)　Watashi no heya wa 5-kai desu.　　(×)

2)　Watashi no heya wa ōkii desu.　Soshite kirei desu.　　(×)

3)　Sentā no shokudō ni iroirona kuni no ryōri ga arimasu.　　(○)

4)　Mainichi Sentā no chikaku no resutoran de gohan o tabemasu.　　(×)

5)　Sentā no chikaku ni sūpā ya kōen ga arimasu.　　(×)

Dai 11 ka

Bunkei

1. Ringo o mittsu kaimasu.
2. Konpyūtā ga 2-dai arimasu.
3. Rao-san wa Nihon ni 1-nen imasu.

Reibun

1. Kyōshitsu ni tsukue ga ikutsu arimasu ka.
   ···Nanatsu arimasu.

2. Kazoku wa nan-nin desu ka.
   ···4-nin desu.

3. Lee-san wa kodomo ga nan-nin imasu ka.
   ···Futari imasu.

4. 80-en no kitte o 5-mai kudasai.
   ···Hai.   Zenbu de 400-en desu.

5. Maiban nan-kai tēpu o kikimasu ka.
   ···2-kai kikimasu.

6. Kuni de donokurai Nihon-go o benkyō-shimashita ka.
   ···3-shūkan dake benkyō-shimashita.

7. Tōkyō kara Ōsaka made shinkansen de donokurai kakarimasu ka.
   ···3-jikan gurai kakarimasu.

Kaiwa

Yūbinkyoku de

Rao   : Sumimasen.

           Kono tegami wa Indo made ikura desu ka.

Kyokuin : 80-en desu.

Rao   : Sorekara kono nimotsu mo onegai-shimasu.

parcel/luggage.

Kyokuin : Ea-mēru desu ka.

Rao   : Ē.

Kyokuin : 2,700-en desu.

Rao   : Donokurai kakarimasu ka.

Kyokuin : 1-shūkan gurai desu.

Renshū A

1. Ringo ga | hitotsu | arimasu.
    | yattsu
    | tō
    | **ikutsu** ············· ka.

2. Kenshūsei ga | hitori | imasu.
    | futari
    | 3-nin
    | **nan-nin** ········· ka.

3. 80-en no kitte o | 1-mai | kudasai.
    | 2-mai
    | 3-mai

4. Watashi wa Ōsaka de | 5-shūkan | jisshū-shimasu.
    | 6-kagetsu
    | 1-nen

    Anata wa ············ | **donokurai** ····················· ka.

5. Watashi no kuni kara Nihon made | 4-jikan | kakarimasu.
    | 5-jikan han
    | 12-jikan

    Anata no ····························· | **donokurai** ·············· ka.

Renshū B

1. Rei : Ringo ga ikutsu arimasu ka. ……Mittsu arimasu.
   1) Tsukue ga ikutsu arimasu ka. ……
   2) Haizara ga ikutsu arimasu ka. ……
   3) Tamago ga ikutsu arimasu ka. ……
   4) Isu ga ikutsu arimasu ka. ……

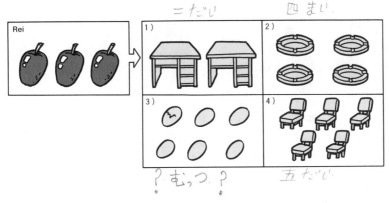

2. Rei : Kazoku wa nan-nin desu ka. (6) ……6-nin desu.
   1) Kyōdai wa nan-nin desu ka. (4) ……
   2) Kodomo wa nan-nin desu ka. (2) ……
   3) Tai no kenshūsei wa nan-nin desu ka. (1) ……
   4) Kenshūsei wa zenbu de nan-nin desu ka. (10) ……

3. Rei : Kikai ga nan-dai arimasu ka. (30) ……30-dai arimasu.
   1) Kitte ga nan-mai arimasu ka. (5) ……
   2) Jidōsha ga nan-dai arimasu ka. (2) ……
   3) Fūtō ga nan-mai arimasu ka. (9) ……
   4) Konpyūtā ga nan-dai arimasu ka. (4) ……

4. Rei : kenshūsei ga imasu ······Kenshūsei ga futari imasu.

   1) terebi ga arimasu ······
   2) kippu o kaimashita ······
   3) mikan o tabemashita ······
   4) 60-en no kitte o kudasai ······

5. Rei : ano eiga o mimashita (2-kai) ······Ano eiga o 2-kai mimashita.

   1) kinō tēpu o kikimashita (4-kai) ······
   2) kono hon o yomimashita (3-kai) ······
   3) senshū Tōkyō e ikimashita (2-kai) ······
   4) kuni ni denwa o kakemashita (1-kai) ······

6. Rei : mainichi hatarakimasu (8-jikan) ······Mainichi 8-jikan hatarakimasu.

   1) raigetsu kara jisshū-shimasu (3-kagetsu) ······
   2) kaisha o yasumimashita (1-shūkan) ······
   3) kuni de Nihon-go o benkyō-shimashita (1-nen) ······
   4) Nagoya ni imasu (mikka) ······

7. Rei : Donokurai Nihon ni imasu ka. (1-nen) ······1-nen imasu.

   1) Maiban nan-jikan benkyō-shimasu ka. (3-jikan) ······
   2) Uchi kara kaisha made donokurai kakarimasu ka. (30-pun gurai) ······
   3) Kōjō de donokurai jisshū-shimasu ka. (6-kagetsu gurai) ······
   4) Kyōto ni nan-nichi imasu ka. (1-nichi dake) ······

Renshū C

1.　A :　Kono ringo wa ikura desu ka.

　　B :　Hitotsu <u>200-en</u> desu.
　　　　　　　　①

　　A :　Ja, <u>mittsu</u> kudasai.
　　　　　　　②

　　B :　Hai.　Zenbu de 600-en desu.

　　　　1)　① 100-en　　② muttsu

　　　　2)　① 150-en　　② yottsu

　　　　3)　① 300-en　　② futatsu

2.　A :　Kazoku wa nan-nin desu ka.

　　B :　<u>4-nin</u> desu.
　　　　　①
　　　　Kanai to kodomo ga <u>futari</u> imasu.
　　　　　　　　　　　　　　②

　　　　1)　① 5-nin　　② 3-nin

　　　　2)　① 3-nin　　② hitori

　　　　3)　① 6-nin　　② 4-nin

3.　A :　Kono tegami wa <u>Tai</u> made ikura desu ka.
　　　　　　　　　　　①

　　B :　80-en desu.

　　A :　Donokurai kakarimasu ka.

　　B :　<u>1-shūkan</u> gurai desu.
　　　　　②

　　　　1)　① Indo　　② 2-shūkan

　　　　2)　① Kankoku　　② itsuka

　　　　3)　① Indoneshia　　② tōka

Mondai

1. 1) _____

    2) _____

    3) _____

    4) _____

    5) _____

2.

1) Kono ringo wa $\left\{\begin{array}{l}\text{a. hitotsu} \\ \text{b. futatsu} \\ \text{c. mittsu}\end{array}\right\}$ 100-en desu.

   Zenbu de (   )-en desu.

2) Lee-san no kazoku wa $\left\{\begin{array}{l}\text{a. hitori} \\ \text{b. futari} \\ \text{c. 4-nin}\end{array}\right\}$ desu.

   (   ) ga $\left\{\begin{array}{l}\text{a. hitori} \\ \text{b. futari} \\ \text{c. 5-nin}\end{array}\right\}$ imasu.

3) (   ) no kitte o $\left\{\begin{array}{l}\text{a. 3-mai} \\ \text{b. 4-mai} \\ \text{c. 5-mai}\end{array}\right\}$ kaimashita.

4) Lee-san wa (   ) de $\left\{\begin{array}{l}\text{a. 1-kagetsu} \\ \text{b. 2-kagetsu} \\ \text{c. 3-kagetsu}\end{array}\right\}$ Nihon-go o naraimashita.

5) Kaisha made (   ) de $\left\{\begin{array}{l}\text{a. 1-jikan} \\ \text{b. 1-jikan han} \\ \text{c. 2-jikan}\end{array}\right\}$ gurai kakarimasu.

3.　Rei :　Fūtō o (1 ··· ichi-mai) kudasai.

　1)　Uchi ni terebi ga (2 ··· 二だい) arimasu.

　2)　60-en no kitte o (4 ··· 四まい) kudasai.

　3)　Ringo o (6 ··· むっつ) kaimashita. (人)

　4)　Kono kōjō ni hito ga (1,000 ··· 千にん) gurai imasu.

　5)　Watashi no kyōdai wa (3 ···三にん(人)) desu.
　　　Imōto ga (2··· ふたり) to, otōto ga (1 ··· ひとり) imasu.

4.　1)　Lee-san wa okusan to kodomo ga futari imasu.　Lee-san no kazoku wa
　　　zenbu de nan-nin desu ka. ······ (四にんです。)

　2)　Kinō mikan o tō kaimashita.　Kesa mittsu tabemashita.　Ima mikan ga
　　　ikutsu arimasu ka. ······ (ななつあります。)

　3)　80-en no kitte o 5-mai to 40-en no kitte o 3-mai kudasai.
　　　Zenbu de ikura desu ka. ······ (五百二十円)です。

　4)　Han-san wa Kenshū Sentā de 6-shūkan benkyō-shimashita.　Korekara
　　　kaisha de 3-kagetsu jisshū-shimasu.　Han-san wa zenbu de donokurai
　　　Nihon ni imasu ka. ······(四かげつ 二)しゅうかん　います。
　　　　　　　　　　　　　　　　(半・はん)

5.　　Watashi wa Narong desu.　Kotoshi 5-gatsu ni Tai kara kimashita.　Ima
　Kenshū Sentā ni imasu.　Sentā ni iroirona kuni no kenshūsei ga imasu.　Ima
　zenbu de 170-nin gurai imasu.　Tai no kenshūsei wa 15-nin desu.
　　Watashi wa kono Sentā de 6-shūkan benkyō-shimasu.　Sorekara Nagoya no
　kaisha de jisshū-shimasu.　Nihon ni 1-nen gurai imasu.　Soshite rainen 4-gatsu
　ni kuni e kaerimasu.

　Rei :　Narong-san wa Tai-jin desu.　　　(○)
　　　　Narong-san wa Marēshia-jin desu.　　(×)

　1)　Sentā ni iroirona kuni no hito ga imasu.　(○)

　2)　Tai no hito ga 170-nin imasu.　(×)

　3)　Narong-san wa Tōkyō de jisshū-shimasu.　(×)

　4)　Narong-san wa kotoshi 5-gatsu ni Nihon e kimashita.　(○)

　5)　Narong-san wa Nihon de 6-kagetsu jisshū-shimasu.　(×)

Dai 12 ka

Bunkei

1. Kinō wa ame deshita.

2. Kinō wa samukatta desu.

3. Tōkyō wa Ōsaka yori ōkii desu.

4. Kurasu de Narong-san ga ichiban wakai desu.

Reibun

1. Kinō wa hima deshita ka.

   ···Hai, hima deshita.

   ···Iie, hima dewa arimasendeshita.

2. Ryokō wa tanoshikatta desu ka.

   ···Hai, tanoshikatta desu.

   ···Iie, tanoshikunakatta desu.

3. Tenki wa yokatta desu ka.

   ···Iie, amari yokunakatta desu.

4. Kinō no eiga wa dō deshita ka.

   ···Totemo omoshirokatta desu.

5. Indo wa Nihon yori atsui desu ka.

   ···Hai, zutto atsui desu.

6. Shinkansen to hikōki to, dochira ga hayai desu ka.

   ···Hikōki no hō ga hayai desu.

7. Niku to sakana to, dochira ga suki desu ka.

   ···Dochira mo suki desu.

8. Supōtsu [no naka] de nani ga ichiban suki desu ka.

   ···Sakkā ga ichiban suki desu.

Kaiwa

Ryokō

Rao   : Tadaima.

Kimura : Okaerinasai.

            Ryokō wa dō deshita ka.

Rao   : Tanoshikatta desu.   Demo, chotto tsukaremashita.

Kimura : Tenki wa dō deshita ka.

Rao   : Sukoshi samukatta desu ga, totemo ii tenki deshita.

Kimura : Doko ga yokatta desu ka.

Rao   : Sō desu ne.   Kyōto ga ichiban yokatta desu.

Renshū A

1. Kinō wa   ame deshita.

                   hima deshita.

                   samukatta desu.

2. yasumi deshita   yasumi dewa arimasendeshita.

   kirei deshita   ⟶   kirei dewa arimasendeshita.

   shizuka deshita   shizuka dewa arimasendeshita.

3. atsu katta desu   atsu kunakatta desu

   oishi katta desu   ⟶   oishi kunakatta desu

   yo katta desu   yo kunakatta desu

4. Tōkyō wa   Ōsaka   yori hito ga ōi desu.

               Yokohama

               Nagoya

5. Densha to basu to, dochira ga   hayai   desu ka.

                                 yasui

   ······Densha no hō ga   hayai   desu.

                            yasui

6. Kurasu de dare ga ichiban   wakai   desu ka.

                           pinpon ga jōzu

   ······Narong-san ga ichiban   wakai   desu.

                           pinpon ga jōzu

Renshū B

1. Rei 1 : ame desu (kinō) ······Kinō wa ame deshita.
   Rei 2 : atsui desu (kinō) ······Kinō wa atsukatta desu.
   1) hima desu (senshū) ······
   2) isogashii desu (sengetsu) ······
   3) ii tenki desu (kinō) ······
   4) atatakai desu (ototoi) ······
   5) yasumi desu (kinō) ······

2. Rei 1 : Lee-san wa genki deshita ka.
   ······Iie, genki dewa arimasendeshita.
   Rei 2 : Shiken wa muzukashikatta desu ka.
   ······Iie, muzukashikunakatta desu.
   1) Kyōto wa shizuka deshita ka. ······
   2) Kinō wa samukatta desu ka. ······
   3) Bangohan wa oishikatta desu ka. ······
   4) Ano mise wa kirei deshita ka. ······
   5) Kinō no pātii wa tanoshikatta desu ka. ······

3. Rei : Kyōto wa dō deshita ka. (totemo kirei) ······Totemo kirei deshita.
   1) Kōgi wa dō deshita ka. (totemo omoshiroi) ······
   2) Ryokō wa dō deshita ka. (totemo tanoshii) ······
   3) Tenki wa dō deshita ka. (amari yokunai) ······
   4) Nara wa dō deshita ka. (totemo shizuka) ······
   5) Shiken wa dō deshita ka. (amari muzukashikunai) ······

12

4. Rei : Tai, Nihon, atsui ……Tai wa Nihon yori atsui desu.

　1) 9-gatsu, 8-gatsu, suzushii ……

　2) Tōkyō, Ōsaka, hito ga ōi ……

　3) Rao-san, Lee-san, wakai ……

　4) Chūgoku, Nihon, ōkii ……

　5) Han-san, Narong-san, Nihon-go ga jōzu ……

5. Rei : Ringo to mikan to, dochira ga suki desu ka. (ringo)
　　　　……Ringo no hō ga suki desu.

　1) Hikōki to shinkansen to, dochira ga hayai desu ka. (hikōki) ……

　2) Indo to Tai to, dochira ga chikai desu ka. (Tai) ……

　3) Do-yōbi to nichi-yōbi to, dochira ga hima desu ka. (nichi-yōbi) ……

　4) Kōhii to kōcha to, dochira ga ii desu ka. (kōhii) ……

　5) Tai-ryōri to Indo-ryōri to, dochira ga karai desu ka. (dochira mo) ……

6. Rei : Supōtsu de nani ga ichiban suki desu ka. (tenisu)
　　　　……Tenisu ga ichiban suki desu.

　1) Kudamono de nani ga ichiban suki desu ka. (ringo) ……

　2) Kurasu de dare ga ichiban wakai desu ka. (Narong-san) ……

　3) Anata no kuni de itsu ga ichiban atsui desu ka. (8-gatsu) ……

　4) Nihon de doko ga ichiban kirei desu ka. (Kyōto) ……

　5) Kengaku de doko ga ichiban yokatta desu ka. (Nagoya-jidōsha) ……

Renshū C

1. A : <u>Kengaku</u> wa dō deshita ka.

①

   B : Totemo <u>omoshirokatta desu.</u>

②

   Demo, chotto tsukaremashita.

   1) ① ryokō   ② ii desu

   2) ① Kyōto   ② kirei desu

   3) ① pātii   ② tanoshii desu

2. A : Nomimono wa ikaga desu ka.

   B : Hai.   Arigatō gozaimasu.

   A : <u>Kōhii</u> to <u>kōcha</u> to, dochira ga ii desu ka.

①   ②

   B : Sō desu ne.   <u>Kōhii</u> o kudasai.

           ①

   1) ① biiru   ② o-sake

   2) ① ocha   ② kōcha

   3) ① jūsu   ② biiru

3. A : Ryokō de doko ga ichiban yokatta desu ka.

   B : Sō desu ne.   <u>Ginza</u> ga ichiban yokatta desu.

           ①

   <u>Ii mise ga ōkatta desu</u> kara.

②

   1) ① Nara   ② totemo shizuka desu

   2) ① Kyōto   ② totemo kirei desu

   3) ① Ōsaka   ② yasui mise ga ōi desu

Mondai

1. 1) _____
   2) _____
   3) _____
   4) _____
   5) _____

2.

1) Chūgoku wa (   ) yori $\begin{cases} \text{a. suzushii} \\ \text{b. samukunai} \\ \text{c. zutto samui} \end{cases}$ desu.

2) Lee-san wa $\begin{cases} \text{a. sakana} \\ \text{b. niku} \\ \text{c. yasai} \end{cases}$ no hō ga suki desu.

   Narong-san wa (   ) mo suki desu.

3) Tai wa (   ) ga ichiban ii desu. $\begin{cases} \text{a. Ichiban atsui} \\ \text{b. Suzushikunai} \\ \text{c. Atsukunai} \end{cases}$ desu kara.

4) Fujisan no (   ) wa $\begin{cases} \text{a. yokatta} \\ \text{b. amari yokunakatta} \\ \text{c. taihen warukatta} \end{cases}$ desu.

5) Pātii wa totemo (   ) desu.

   Ryōri de $\begin{cases} \text{a. Indo-ryōri} \\ \text{b. Nihon-ryōri} \\ \text{c. Tai-ryōri} \end{cases}$ ga ichiban oishikatta desu.

3. Rei : ōkii ······ (chiisai)   4) chikai ······ (とおい)
   1) hayai ······ (おそい)   5) amai ······ (からい)
   2) ii ······ (わるい)   6) isogashii ······ (ひま (な))
   3) ōi ······ (すくない)   7) suzushii ······ (あたたかい)
            (小ない)

4.

Rei : atsui desu	atsukunai desu	atsukatta desu	atsukunakatta desu
muzukashii desu	むずかしくない～	むずかしかった～	むずかしくなかった～
omoshiroi desu	おもしろくない～	おもしろかった～	おもしろくなかった～
ii desu	よくない～	よかった～	よくなかった～
hima desu	ひまではありません。	ひまでした	ひまではありませんでした。
ame desu	あめではありません。	あめでした	あめではありませんでした。

5. Rei : Kore wa [nan] desu ka. ……Sore wa hon desu.

1) Kōhii to kōcha to, [どちら] ga suki desu ka.

　　……Dochira mo suki desu.

2) Nihon de [いつ / 何月] ga ichiban samui desu ka.

　　……2-gatsu ga ichiban samui desu.

3) Kurasu de [だれ / どちら] ga ichiban wakai desu ka.

　　……Narong-san ga ichiban wakai desu.

4) Kudamono de [何 / なに] ga ichiban suki desu ka.

　　……Ringo ga ichiban suki desu.

5) Nihon de [どこ] ga ichiban kirei desu ka.

　　……Kyōto ga ichiban kirei desu.

6) Tōkyō to Ōsaka to, [どちら] ga hito ga ōi desu ka.

　　……Tōkyō no hō ga zutto ōi desu.

7) Kesa no shiken wa [どう] deshita ka.

　　……Amari muzukashikunakatta desu.

6.

　Kinō watashi wa Fujisan e (Rei : ikimasu …ikimashita).　Fujisan wa
Nihon de ichiban takai yama desu.　3,776 m (mētoru) desu.
Watashi wa ichiban ue made ikimashita.　Hito ga taihen (ōi desu … 多かったです(おおい)).
Tenki ga (ii desu … よかったです) kara, totemo (kirei desu … きれいでした).
Demo, sukoshi (samui desu … さむかったで).　Chotto tsukaremashita ga,
totemo (tanoshii desu…たのしかった)です。

Fujisan　3,776m

Dai 13 ka

Bunkei

1. Watashi wa kamera ga hoshii desu.

2. Watashi wa eiga o mitai desu.
   (ga)
3. Watashi wa depāto e kutsu o kai ni ikimasu.

Reibun

1. Ima nani ga ichiban hoshii desu ka.

   ···Jidōsha ga hoshii desu.

2. Nani o kaitai desu ka.

   ···Bideo o kaitai desu.

3. Nanika nomitai desu ne.

   ···Sō desu ne.   Nani o nomitai desu ka.

   Biiru o nomitai desu.

4. Konban Shinjuku e ikimasen ka.

   ···Tsukaremashita kara, doko mo ikitakunai desu.

5. Doko e ikimasu ka.

   ···Yokohama e eiga o mi ni ikimasu.

6. Gogo wa itsumo kōgi desu ka.

   ···Iie, tokidoki kōjō e kengaku ni ikimasu.

7. Tōkyō e nani o shi ni ikimasu ka.

   ···Tomodachi no uchi e asobi ni ikimasu.

8. Nihon e nan no jisshū ni kimashita ka.

   ···Konpyūtā no jisshū ni kimashita.

Kaiwa

Gaishutsu

Han : Ii tenki desu ne.

Rao : Ē.　Dokoka ikitai desu ne.

Han : Yokohama-kōen e asobi ni ikimasen ka.

Rao : Ii desu ne.

Rao : Kireina kōen desu ne.

Han : Sō desu ne.　···A, mō 12-ji desu yo.

Rao : Onaka ga sukimashita ne.

Han : Watashi wa nodo ga kawakimashita.

Rao : Ano resutoran ni hairimasen ka.

Han : Ē, sō shimashō.

Renshū A

1.

masu-kei		
I	nomi	masu
	kai	masu
	kaeri	masu
	asobi	masu

masu-kei		
II	tabe	masu
	kae	masu
	ne	masu
	mi	masu

masu-kei		
III	ki	masu
	shi	masu
	jisshū-shi	masu
	kaimono-shi	masu

2. Watashi wa

jisho
jidōsha
tomodachi

ga hoshii desu.

3. Watashi wa

hon o | yomi | tai desu.
Tōkyō e | iki
depāto de | kaimono-shi

Anata wa | nani o shi ············ ka.

4.

iki tai desu
tabe tai desu
benkyō-shi tai desu

⟶

iki takunai desu
tabe takunai desu
benkyō-shi takunai desu

5. Watashi wa   Ginza e

| asobi | ni ikimasu.
eiga o | mi
nekutai o | kai

Anata wa ········· | nani o shi ··············· ka.

6. Watashi wa Yokohama e

kaimono
kenbutsu
denki no jisshū

ni ikimasu.

Renshū B

1. Rei : ⋯⋯Watashi wa kamera ga hoshii desu.
   ☞ 1) ⋯⋯
   2) ⋯⋯
   3) ⋯⋯
   4) ⋯⋯
   5) ⋯⋯

2. Rei : Donna terebi ga hoshii desu ka. (ōkii) ⋯⋯Ōkii terebi ga hoshii desu.
   1) Donna rajikase ga hoshii desu ka.(chiisai) ⋯⋯
   2) Donna kamera ga hoshii desu ka. (Mirion no) ⋯⋯
   3) Donna bideo ga hoshii desu ka. (yasui) ⋯⋯
   4) Donna kuruma ga hoshii desu ka. (Nagoya-jidōsha no) ⋯⋯

3. Rei : gohan o tabemasu ⋯⋯Gohan o tabetai desu.
   1) terebi o mimasu ⋯⋯
   2) kōhii o nomimasu ⋯⋯
   3) omiyage o kaimasu ⋯⋯
   4) konpyūtā o benkyō-shimasu ⋯⋯
   5) tomodachi ni aimasu ⋯⋯
   6) kuni e kaerimasu ⋯⋯
   7) rainen kekkon-shimasu ⋯⋯
   8) Indo ni nimotsu o okurimasu ⋯⋯

4. Rei : Nani o kaitai desu ka. (bideo) ⋯⋯Bideo o kaitai desu.
   1) Nani o nomitai desu ka. (biiru) ⋯⋯
   2) Nichi-yōbi doko e ikitai desu ka. (Ginza) ⋯⋯
   3) Doko o kengaku-shitai desu ka. (Nagoya-jidōsha) ⋯⋯
   4) Nani o tabetai desu ka. (nani mo) ⋯⋯

13

5. Rei 1 : Shinjuku e ikimasu, kamera o kaimasu
        ······Shinjuku e kamera o kai ni ikimasu.
   Rei 2 : kōjō e ikimasu, kengaku-shimasu
        ······Kōjō e kengaku ni ikimasu.
   1) ginkō e ikimasu, okane o kaemasu ······
   2) itsumo kōen e ikimasu, sanpo-shimasu ······
   3) resutoran e ikimasu, kōhii o nomimasu ······
   4) Nihon e kimashita, benkyō-shimasu ······

6. Rei : Doko e omiyage o kai ni ikimasu ka. (depāto)
        ······Depāto e kai ni ikimasu.
   1) Doko e eiga o mi ni ikimasu ka. (Ginza) ······
   2) Doko e kengaku ni ikimasu ka. (Tōkyō-denki) ······
   3) Nichi-yōbi doko e asobi ni ikimasu ka. (Kyōto) ······
   4) Raishū kara doko e jisshū ni ikimasu ka. (Hiroshima) ······

7. Rei : Depāto e nani o shi ni ikimashita ka. ······Kaimono ni ikimashita.
   1) Ginkō e nani o shi ni ikimashita ka. ······
   2) Tōkyō e nani o shi ni ikimashita ka. ······
   3) Shinjuku e nani o shi ni ikimashita ka. ······
   4) Nihon e nani o shi ni kimashita ka. ······

Renshū C

1. A : Ii <u>kamera</u> desu ne.

    B : Ē, kinō Shinjuku de kaimashita.

    A : Sō desu ka.　Watashi mo <u>kamera</u> ga hoshii desu.

    1)　tokei

    2)　sutereo

    3)　rajikase

2. A : <u>Nodo ga kawakimashita</u> ne.
    　　①
    B : Ē, <u>nanika nomitai</u> desu ne.
    　　②
    A : Ano resutoran ni hairimasen ka.

    B : Ē, sō shimashō.

    1)　① onaka ga sukimashita

    　　② nanika tabemasu

    2)　① tsukaremashita

    　　② chotto yasumimasu

    3)　① nodo ga kawakimashita

    　　② biiru o nomimasu

3. A : Doko e ikimasu ka.

    B : <u>Depāto</u> e <u>kaimono</u> ni ikimasu.
    　　①　　　　②
    A : Sō desu ka.　Itte irasshai.

    1)　① Yokohama

    　　② eiga o mimasu

    2)　① tomodachi no uchi

    　　② asobimasu

    3)　① Shinjuku

    　　② kamera o kaimasu

Mondai

1.　1)　_____
　　2)　_____
　　3)　_____
　　4)　_____
　　5)　_____

2.

1)　Watashi wa ⎰ a. ii ⎱ (　　　　) ga hoshii desu.
　　　　　　　 ⎱ b. yasui ⎰
　　　　　　　 c. chiisai

2)　⎰ a. Sakana ga suki desu ⎱
　　⎰ b. Onaka ga sukimashita ⎰ kara, (　　　　) o tabetai desu.
　　 c. Nodo ga kawakimashita

3)　Onaka ga ⎰ a. sukimashita ⎱ kara, (　　　　) tabetakunai desu.
　　　　　　 ⎱ b. ippai desu ⎰
　　　　　　 c. itai desu

4)　Korekara (　　　　) e ⎰ a. eiga o mi ⎱ ni ikimasu.
　　　　　　　　　　　　　 ⎱ b. o-sake o nomi ⎰
　　　　　　　　　　　　　 c. gohan o tabe

5)　(　　　　) no gogo Tōkyō-denki e ⎰ a. kenbutsu ⎱ ni ikimasu.
　　　　　　　　　　　　　　　　　　 ⎱ b. kengaku ⎰
　　　　　　　　　　　　　　　　　　 c. jisshū

3.　Rei :　Ii tenki desu kara, dokoka (　iki　) tai desu.
　　1)　Nodo ga kawakimashita kara, mizu o (飲み) tai desu.
　　2)　Onaka ga sukimashita kara, nanika (食べ) tai desu.
　　3)　Tsukaremashita kara, chotto (休み) tai desu.
　　4)　Kyō wa samui desu kara, doko mo (行き) takunai desu.
　　5)　Onaka ga ippai desu kara, nani mo (食べ) takunai desu.

4. Rei : Resutoran e gohan o (tabe) ni ikimasu.

1) Ashita Ginza e eiga o (見) ni ikimasu.

2) Ginkō e okane o (かえ) ni ikimasu.

3) Maiasa kōen e (さんぽ) ni ikimasu.

4) Nichi-yōbi tomodachi to depāto e (買物) ni ikimasu.

5) Kinō wa hima deshita kara, tomodachi no uchi e (あそび) ni ikimashita.

5. Rei : [Doko] (e) ikimasu ka. ······Kyōto e ikimasu.

1) [何] (が) hoshii desu ka. ······Bideo ga hoshii desu.

2) [どんな] sutereo ga hoshii desu ka.
······Chiisai sutereo ga hoshii desu.

3) [どこ] (へ) ikitai desu ka. ······Kyōto e ikitai desu.

4) [何] (を) nomitai desu ka. ······Kōhii o nomitai desu.

5) [だれ] (に) ichiban aitai desu ka. ······Kodomo ni aitai desu.

6) Shinjuku e [何] (を) shi ni ikimasu ka.
······Kamera o kai ni ikimasu.

7) Nihon e [何] (の) jisshū ni kimashita ka.
······Konpyūtā no jisshū ni kimashita.

6. Rei : Gohan (o) tabemasu.

Kinō wa yasumi deshita kara, watashi wa Lee-san to Shinjuku (へ)
asobi (に) ikimashita. Shinjuku wa totemo nigiyakana machi deshita.
Eki no chikaku (に) iroirona mise ga arimashita. Watashi-tachi wa
ōkii kamera-ya (に) hairimashita. Lee-san wa kono mise (で) Mirion
no kamera (を) kaimashita. Watashi mo kamera (が) hoshikatta desu.
Demo, okane (が) arimasendeshita kara, nani (を) kaimasendeshita.

Fukushū B

1.

Rei 1 : shizuka desu	shizuka dewa arimasen	shizuka deshita	shizuka dewa arimasendeshita
Rei 2 :　atsui desu	atsukunai desu	atsukatta desu	atsukunakatta desu
kirei desu	きれいではありません	きれいでした	きれいではありませんでした
oishii desu	おいしくないです。	おいしかったです。	おいしくなかったです。
nigiyaka desu	にぎやかではありません	にぎやかでした	にぎやかではありませんでした
samui desu	さむくないです。	さむかったです。	さむくなかったです。
ii desu	よくないです	よかったです。	よくなかったです。
hima desu	ひまではありません	ひまでした。	ひまではありませんでした
genki desu	げんきではありません	げんきでした。	げんきではありませんでした
hayai desu	はやくないです。	はやかったです。	はやくなかったです。
tanoshii desu	たのしくないです。	たのしかったです	たのしくなかったです。
tōi desu	とうくないです	とうかったです	とうくなかったです。

2.　Rei :　Ano hito wa [　dare　] desu ka. ……Rao-san desu.

1)　[　何　] de jidōsha o shūri-shimasu ka.

　　……Doraibā to supana de shūri-shimasu.

2)　[　だれ　] ni tegami o kakimasu ka. ……Kazoku ni kakimasu.

3)　Nihon-go wa [　どう　] desu ka.

　　……Muzukashii desu ga, omoshiroi desu.

4)　Kyōto wa [　どんな　] machi desu ka. ……Kireina machi desu.

5)　Lee-san no kaban wa [　どれ　] desu ka.

　　……Ano kuroi kaban desu.

6)　[　何の　] supōtsu ga suki desu ka. ……Tenisu ga suki desu.

7)　[　なぜ / どうして　] gohan o tabemasen ka. ……Onaka ga ippai desu kara.

8)　Jimusho ni [　だれ　] ga imasu ka. ……Tanaka-san ga imasu.

9)　Tsukue no naka ni [　何　] ga arimasu ka.

　　……Hasami ya hotchikisu ga arimasu.

10)　Ginkō wa [　どこ　] ni arimasu ka. ……Eki no chikaku ni arimasu.

11)　Kono tegami wa Indo made [　いくら　] desu ka.……80-en desu.

12)　Ringo o [　いくつ　] kaimashita ka. ……Itsutsu kaimashita.

13)　Kazoku wa [　何人　] desu ka. ……5-nin desu.

14) Tōkyō kara Ōsaka made [どのくらい] kakarimasu ka.

······Shinkansen de 3-jikan desu.

15) Nihon de [どのくらい] jisshū-shimasu ka.

······4-kagetsu gurai jisshū-shimasu.

16) Kōjō ni kikai ga [何だい] arimasu ka. ······30-dai arimasu.

3.　Rei :　Watashi (　wa　) Rao desu.

1) Hasami (で) kami o kirimasu.

2) Nihon-go (で) repōto o kakimasu.

3) Watashi wa tomodachi (に) denwa o kakemasu.

4) Watashi wa Lee-san (から) purezento o moraimashita.

5) Nihon no tabemono wa oishii desu (が),takai desu.

6) Watashi wa tamago (が) suki desu.　Mainichi tamago

(を) tabemasu.

7) Rao-san wa pinpon (が) jōzu desu.

8) Kuni de Nihon-go (を) benkyō-shimashita.

9) Nihon-go (が) sukoshi wakarimasu.

10) Tanaka-san wa jidōsha (が) arimasu.

11) Onaka (が) itai desu (から), heya de yasumimasu.

12) Tsukue (の) ue (に) kaban ga arimasu.

13) Heya (に) iroirona mono (が) arimasu.

Tsukue (や) beddo (など) arimasu.

14) Ali-san (は) doko desu ka. ······Robii (に) imasu.

15) Kōhii (と) kōcha (と), dochira (が) ii desu ka.

16) Narong-san (は) wakai desu.

Kurasu (で) Narong-san (が) ichiban wakai desu.

17) Supōtsu (で) sakkā (が) ichiban suki desu.

18) Watashi wa ii kamera (が) hoshii desu.

19) Yokohama (で) eiga o mimashita.

20) Yokohama (へ) eiga o mi (に) ikimashita.

21) Nihon (で) kikai (を) jisshū-shimasu.

22) Nihon (に) kikai (を) jisshū (に) kimashita.

23) Nihon (に) 1-nen imasu.

24) Maiasa kōen (で) sanpo-shimasu.

25) Raigetsu Sentā (に) demasu.

B

111

Dai 14 ka

Bunkei

1. Jisho o kashite kudasai.
2. Lee-san wa ima terebi o mite imasu.

Reibun

1. Wakarimasu ka.

   ···Iie, wakarimasen.　Yukkuri hanashite kudasai.

2. Sumimasen ga, chotto haizara o totte kudasai.

   ···Hai, dōzo.

3. Jikan ga arimasen kara, isoide kudasai.

   ···Chotto matte kudasai.　Sugu ikimasu.

4. Wāpuro no tsukai-kata ga wakarimasu ka.

   ···Iie, wakarimasen.　Sumimasen ga, oshiete kudasai.

5. Tēpu-rekōdā o misete kudasai.

   ···Donna tēpu-rekōdā ga ii desu ka.

   Chiisai no o misete kudasai.

6. Ima nani o shite imasu ka.

   ···Shukudai o shite imasu.

   Ja, mata ato de kimasu.

7. Ame ga futte imasu ne.　Takushii o yobimashō ka.

   ···Hai, yonde kudasai.

Kaiwa

Kamera-ya de

Ten'in : Irasshaimase.

Rao : Sumimasen. Ano kamera o misete kudasai.

Ten'in : Hai, dōzo.

Rao : Ii kamera desu ga, takai desu ne.

Mō sukoshi yasui no wa arimasen ka.

Ten'in : Kochira wa ikaga desu ka. 30,000-en desu.

Rao : Ūn···sō desu ne.

Dōmo sumimasen. Mata kimasu.

Renshū A

1.

	masu-kei			te-kei		
I	ka	ki	masu	ka	i	te
	*i	ki	masu	i	t	te
	iso	gi	masu	iso	i	de
	no	mi	masu	no	n	de
	yo	bi	masu	yo	n	de
	to	ri	masu	to	t	te
	ka	i	masu	ka	t	te
	ma	chi	masu	ma	t	te
	ka	shi	masu	ka	shi	te

	masu-kei		te-kei	
II	tabe	masu	tabe	te
	ne	masu	ne	te
	oki	masu	oki	te
	kari	masu	kari	te
	mi	masu	mi	te
	i	masu	i	te

	masu-kei		te-kei	
III	ki	masu	ki	te
	shi	masu	shi	te
	shūri-shi	masu	shūri-shi	te

2.

Namae o	kaite	kudasai.
Kotoba o	oboete	
Jimusho e	kite	

3. Tanaka-san wa ima

ongaku o	kiite
kaisha no hito to	hanashite
denwa o	kakete
nani o shite	

imasu.

········· ka.

14

Renshū B

1. Rei : satō o torimasu ······Sumimasen ga, satō o totte kudasai.
   1) kasa o kashimasu ······
   2) yukkuri hanashimasu ······
   3) chotto machimasu ······
   4) takushii o yobimasu ······
   5) mō ichido iimasu ······

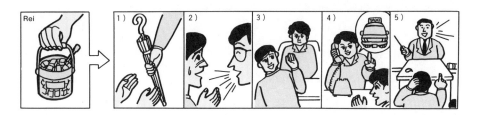

2. Rei : okane ga arimasen, kashimasu
   　　　 ······Okane ga arimasen kara, kashite kudasai.
   1) jikan ga arimasen, isogimasu ······
   2) 9-ji desu, hayaku kyōshitsu e kimasu ······
   3) watashi wa Nihon-go ga yoku wakarimasen, mō sukoshi yukkuri
      hanashimasu ······
   4) ima isogashii desu, ato de kimasu ······
   5) taipu no tsukai-kata ga wakarimasen, oshiemasu ······

3. Rei : Takushii o yobimashō ka. ······Hai, yonde kudasai.
   1) Tetsudaimashō ka. ······
   2) Kasa o kashimashō ka. ······
   3) Shio o torimashō ka. ······
   4) Sentā no jūsho o kakimashō ka. ······
   5) Mō ichido denwa-bangō o iimashō ka. ······

4. Rei : Lee-san wa robii de terebi o mimasu
   ……Lee-san wa ima robii de terebi o mite imasu.

   1) Narong-san wa shokudō de gohan o tabemasu ……
   2) Rao-san wa robii de kaisha no hito to hanashimasu ……
   3) Ali-san wa heya de rajio o kikimasu ……
   4) Kim-san wa niwa de shashin o torimasu ……
   5) Lee-san wa asoko de tenisu o shimasu ……

5. Rei : Ali-san wa nani o shite imasu ka.
   ……Denwa o kakete imasu.

   1) Tanaka-san wa nani o shite imasu ka. ……
   2) Narong-san wa dare to hanashite imasu ka. ……
   3) Rao-san wa terebi o mite imasu ka. ……
   4) Lee-san wa nani o shite imasu ka. ……
   5) Ima ame ga futte imasu ka. ……

Renshū C

1. A : Sumimasen.

   B : Hai.

   A : Chotto <u>bōrupen o kashite</u> kudasai.

   B : Hai, dōzo.

   1) haizara o torimasu
   2) kasa o kashimasu
   3) sono shatsu o misemasu

2. A : Ja, ikimashō.

   A, Rao-san ga imasen ne.

   Nani o shite imasu ka.

   B : <u>Robii de kaisha no hito to hanashite</u> imasu.

   1) niwa de shashin o torimasu
   2) shokudō de gohan o tabemasu
   3) robii de tegami o yomimasu

3. A : Sumimasen ga, chotto wakarimasen.

   B : Ja, <u>mō ichido iimashō</u> ka.

   A : Ē, <u>mō ichido itte</u> kudasai.

   1) rōmaji de kakimasu
   2) Eigo de hanashimasu
   3) mō sukoshi yukkuri iimasu

Mondai

1. 1) _____
   2) _____
   3) _____
   4) _____
   5) _____

2.
   1) Sentā no ( ) wa { a. 768-1621 / b. 786-1621 / c. 861-7621 } desu.

   2) Koko ni bōrupen de ( ) o { a. kaite / b. kashite / c. katte } kudasai.

   3) Mō sukoshi ōkii ( ) wa { a. arimasu. / b. arimasen. / c. imasen. }

   4) Rao-san wa ima ( ) de { a. hon o yonde / b. gohan o tabete / c. ocha o nonde } imasu.

   5) Ame ga { a. sukoshi futte imasu / b. takusan futte imasu / c. amari futte imasen } kara, ( ) o karimashita.

3.

Rei : kakimasu	kaite	torimasu	とって	oboemasu	おぼえて
kikimasu	きって	kaerimasu	かえて	nemasu	ねて
ikimasu	いって	suimasu	すって	(6-ji ni) okimasu	おきて
isogimasu	いそいで	iimasu	いって	mimasu	みって
machimasu	まって	tetsudaimasu	てつだって	imasu	いって
nomimasu	のんで	kashimasu	おして	shimasu	して
yasumimasu	やすんで	tabemasu	たべて	benkyō-shimasu	して
asobimasu	あそいで	kakemasu	かけて	(Nihon e) kimasu	きって

4.　Rei :　Chotto bōrupen o (kashimasu ···　　kashite　　) kudasai.

1)　Taipu no tsukai-kata o (oshiemasu ··· おしえて) kudasai.

2)　Jikan ga arimasen kara, (isogimasu ··· いそいで) kudasai.

3)　Mō 9-ji desu kara, hayaku kyōshitsu ni (hairimasu ··· はいって) kudasai.

4)　Nihon-go ga amari wakarimasen kara, mō sukoshi yukkuri
　　　(hanashimasu ··· はなして) kudasai.

5)　Ima isogashii desu kara, sumimasen ga, mata ato de
　　　(kimasu ··· きて) kudasai.

6)　Ali-san wa ima nani o (shimasu ··· して) imasu ka.
　　　······ Heya de ongaku o (kikimasu ··· きって) imasu.

7)　Takushii o yobimashō ka. ······ Hai, (yobimasu ··· よんで) kudasai.

8)　Tetsudaimashō ka.
　　　······ Hai, sumimasen ga, (tetsudaimasu ··· てつだって) kudasai.

14

119

5.　┌───┐
　　Kyō wa asa kara ame ga futte imasu.　Ima 7-ji han desu.　Watashi wa robii ni
　imasu.　Soshite terebi o mite imasu.　Watashi wa maiasa 7-ji kara terebi o
　mimasu.　Ali-san wa shinbun o yonde imasu.　Lee-san wa mado no chikaku de
　Nihon-go o benkyō-shite imasu.　Maiasa 9-ji kara shiken ga arimasu.　Lee-san wa
　itsumo yoku benkyō-shimasu.
　　└───┘

Rei :　Kyō wa kumori desu.　　　(✕)
　　　Ima 7-ji han desu.　　　(○)

1)　Kyō wa ame desu.　　　(○)

2)　Watashi wa ima shinbun o yonde imasu.　　(✕)

3)　Watashi wa ima robii de terebi o mite imasu.　　(○)

4)　Lee-san wa kyōshitsu de Nihon-go o benkyō-shite imasu.　　(✕)

5)　Lee-san wa ima shiken o shite imasu.　　(✕)

Dai 15 ka

Bunkei

1. Tabako o sutte mo ii desu.
2. Rao-san wa ii kamera o motte imasu.

Reibun

1. Koko ni suwatte mo ii desu ka.
   ···Ē, ii desu yo.   Dōzo.

2. Kono jisho o karite mo ii desu ka.
   ···Sumimasen.   Ima tsukatte imasu kara.

3. Koko de tabako o sutte mo ii desu ka.
   ···Iie, ikemasen.   Kin'en desu kara.

4. Tanaka-san wa doko ni sunde imasu ka.
   ···Tōkyō ni sunde imasu.

5. Sentā no denwa-bangō o shitte imasu ka.
   ···Iie, shirimasen.

6. Suzuki-san wa dokushin desu ka.
   ···Iie, kekkon-shite imasu.

7. O-shigoto wa nan desu ka.
   ···Enjinia desu.
   Jidōsha no kaisha de hataraite imasu.

Kaiwa

Kazoku

Yamamoto : Rao-san wa kekkon-shite imasu ka.

Rao : Iie, dokushin desu.

Kazoku to issho ni sunde imasu.

Yamamoto : Kyōdai wa nan-nin desu ka.

Rao : Imōto ga futari imasu.

Yamamoto : Imōto-san wa o-ikutsu desu ka.

Rao : Ue no imōto wa 21 desu.

Ginkō de hataraite imasu.

Shita no imōto wa 18 desu.

Ima daigaku de benkyō-shite imasu.

Renshū A

1.
Shashin o	totte	mo ii desu ka.
Enpitsu de	kaite	
Kono denwa o	tsukatte	

2.
Watashi wa		kekkon-shite	imasu.
	Yokohama ni	sunde	
	Kimura-san o	shitte	

3.
Ano hito wa	ginkō de	hataraite	imasu.
	daigaku de Eigo o	oshiete	
	daigaku de	benkyō-shite	

Renshū B

1. Rei :　······Tabako o sutte mo ii desu ka.
    1)　······
   2)　······
   3)　······
   4)　······
   5)　······

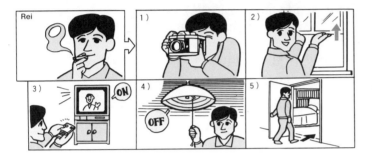

2. Rei :　samui desu,　mado o shimemasu
   　　　　　······Samui desu kara, mado o shimete mo ii desu ka.
   1)　atama ga itai desu,　uchi e kaerimasu ······
   2)　atsui desu,　mado o akemasu ······
   3)　ame ga futte imasu,　kasa o karimasu ······
   4)　bōrupen ga arimasen,　enpitsu de kakimasu ······
   5)　netsu ga arimasu,　kaisha o yasumimasu ······

3. Rei 1 :　Uchi e kaette mo ii desu ka. (hai) ······Hai, ii desu.
   Rei 2 :　Robii de o-sake o nonde mo ii desu ka. (iie) ······Iie, ikemasen.
   1)　Kono taipu o tsukatte mo ii desu ka. (hai) ······
   2)　Koko de tabako o sutte mo ii desu ka. (iie) ······
   3)　Koko ni suwatte mo ii desu ka. (hai) ······
   4)　Kōjō no naka de shashin o totte mo ii desu ka. (iie) ······
   5)　Asoko ni nimotsu o oite mo ii desu ka. (hai) ······

4. Rei : Narong-san wa kekkon-shite imasu ka. (iie)

           ······Iie, kekkon-shite imasen.

1） Kimura-san o shitte imasu ka. (hai) ······

2） Sentā no denwa-bangō o shitte imasu ka. (iie) ······

3） Tēpu-rekōdā o motte imasu ka. (iie) ······

4） Suzuki-san wa kekkon-shite imasu ka. (hai) ······

5） Kazoku to issho ni sunde imasu ka. (iie) ······

15

5. Rei : Doko de yasui kamera o utte imasu ka. (Shinjuku)

           ······Shinjuku de utte imasu.

1） Okusan wa doko de hataraite imasu ka. (byōin) ······

2） Oniisan wa daigaku de nani o oshiete imasu ka. (Eigo) ······

3） Imōto-san wa doko no daigaku de benkyō-shite imasu ka.

    (Tōkyō no daigaku) ······

4） Doko de taoru ya sekken o utte imasu ka. (uketsuke) ······

5） Anata no kaisha wa nani o tsukutte imasu ka. (denki-seihin) ······

Renshū C

1. A : Kono <u>jisho</u> o karite mo ii desu ka.
   B : Ē, ii desu yo.　Dōzo.
   A : Heya de tsukatte mo ii desu ka.
   B : Sumimasen.　Koko de tsukatte kudasai.

   1)　tēpu-rekōdā
   2)　rajikase
   3)　serotēpu

2. A : <u>Kaisha no denwa-bangō</u> o shitte imasu ka.
   B : Ē, shitte imasu yo.
   A : Ja, sumimasen ga, oshiete kudasai.

   1)　Sentā no jūsho
   2)　Kimura-san no uchi
   3)　Rao-san no heya no bangō

3. A : O-shigoto wa nan desu ka.
   B : <u>Enjinia</u> desu.
   　　①
   　　<u>Tōkyō-denki</u> de hataraite imasu.
   　　②

   1)　① kaishain　　② Yokohama-kikai
   2)　① ginkōin　　② Ōsaka-ginkō
   3)　① enjinia　　② konpyūtā no kaisha

Mondai

1. 1) _____

    🔊 2) _____

    3) _____

    4) _____

    5) _____

15

2.

🔊 1) Koko wa (   ) desu kara, { a. koko de sutte mo ii desu. / b. robii de sutte kudasai. / c. asoko de sutte imasu. }

2) Suzuki-san wa { a. dokushin desu. / b. kekkon-shimasu. / c. kekkon-shite imasu. }

    Uchi wa Sentā no (   ) ni arimasu.

126

3) Lee-san wa (   ) o { a. motte imasu. / b. motte imasen. / c. kashimashita. }

4) Lee-san wa Tanaka-san no (   ) o shitte imasu ga,

    denwa-bangō o { a. shirimasen. / b. shite imasen. / c. shitte imasu. }

5) Yamamoto-san wa (   ) desu.

    Yokohama-kikai de { a. tsukutte / b. hataraite / c. utte } imasu.

3. Rei : tabete (tabemasu)

1) kiite (聞きます)　　　　6) keshite (けします)　　11) akete (あけます)

2) kaite (書きます)　　　　7) katte (買います)　　　12) shite (します)

*3) okite (おきます)　　　8) isoide (いそぎます)　　13) ite (います)

4) tatte (たちます)　　　　9) kaette (帰ります)　　*14) oite (おきます)

5) okutte (おくります)　　10) kite (来ます)　　　　15) asonde (あそびます)

* NB// おく = to put ⎫ おきます
      おきる = to get up ⎭

4. Rei : hairimasu ……(demasu)

1) tsukemasu ……(けします)　　　4) agemasu ……(もらいます)

2) akemasu ……(しめます)　　　5) kashimasu ……(かります)

3) tachimasu ……(すわります)　　6) naraimasu ……(教えます)

15

5. Rei : Tēpu o (kikimasu … kiite) kudasai.

1) Samui desu kara, mado o (shimemasu … しめて) kudasai.

2) Sumimasen ga, denki o (tsukemasu … つけて) kudasai.

3) Asoko ni nimotsu o (okimasu … おいて) kudasai.

4) Koko ni (suwarimasu … すわって) mo ii desu ka.

5) Kono hasami o (karimasu … かりて) mo ii desu ka.

6) Lee-san wa ii kamera o (mochimasu … もって) imasu.

6.

Watashi no kazoku wa 4-nin desu. Kanai to kodomo ga futari imasu. Kodomo wa otoko no ko to onna no ko desu. Otoko no ko wa 7-sai desu. Mainichi gakkō de benkyō-shite imasu. Onna no ko wa ima 4-sai desu. Watashi-tachi wa Indo no Delhi ni sunde imasu.

Watashi wa Delhi no jidōsha no kaisha de hataraite imasu. Zenbu de 1,500-nin gurai hito ga hataraite imasu. Seihin no 95% (pāsento) o Indo de utte imasu. Watashi wa kyonen kaisha no kuruma o kaimashita. Chiisai desu ga, totemo ii kuruma desu.

127

Rei : Watashi no kazoku wa 4-nin desu.　　(○)

　　　Watashi no kazoku wa 3-nin desu.　　(×)

1) Futari no kodomo wa gakkō de benkyō-shite imasu.　(×)

2) Watashi wa kazoku to issho ni Indo ni sunde imasu.　(○)

3) Watashi no kaisha wa jidōsha o tsukutte imasu.　(○)

4) Watashi no kaisha wa totemo chiisai kaisha desu.　(×)

5) Seihin no 95% (pāsento) o iroirona kuni e utte imasu.　(×)

6) Watashi wa kuruma o motte imasu.　(○)

Dai 16 ka

Bunkei

1. Asa okite, gohan o tabete, kaisha e ikimasu.

2. Shigoto ga owatte kara, sugu uchi e kaerimasu.

3. Tōkyō wa hito ga ōkute, nigiyaka desu.

多くて
much/many (て form)

Reibun

1. Kinō nani o shimashita ka.

   ···Depāto e itte, kaimono-shite, sorekara 6-ji goro
   Sentā e kaerimashita.

2. Yokohama-kōen made dōyatte ikimasu ka.

   ···Yokohama made densha de itte, 80-ban no basu ni notte,
   Kōen-mae de orimasu.

3. Kōgi ga owatte kara, nani o shimasu ka.
   ···Tomodachi to pinpon o shimasu.

4. Han-san wa dono hito desu ka.
   ···Ano kami ga nagakute, kireina hito desu.

   長くて.

5. Kōbe wa donna machi desu ka.
   ···Kirei de, nigiyakana machi desu.

6. Ano hito wa dare desu ka.
   ···Rao-san desu.   Indo-jin de, Tōkyō-denki no kenshūsei desu.

Kaiwa

Resutoran e iku

Kimura : Benkyō ga owatte kara, issho ni shokuji-shimasen ka.

Narong : Ē, doko e ikimasu ka.

Kimura : Narong-san wa nani ga tabetai desu ka.

Narong : Nan demo ii desu.

Kimura : Ja, yasukute, ii mise ga arimasu kara,
soko e ikimashō.

Kimura : Nan ni shimasu ka.

Narong : Ēto · · ·

Kimura : Kono mise wa hanbāgu ga oishii desu yo.

Narong : Ja, sore ni shimasu.

Kimura : Sumimasen. Hanbāgu o futatsu onegai-shimasu.

Renshū A

1.

Asa	okite,	kao o		aratte,	gohan o tabemasu.
Ginza e	itte,	tomodachi ni		atte,	eiga o mimashita.
Terebi o	mite,	Nihon-go o	benkyō-shite,		sorekara nemashita.

2.

Hirugohan o	tabete	kara,	sukoshi yasumimasu.
Shigoto ga	owatte		eiga o mimasu.
Shawā o	abite		nemashita.

3.

Ano hito wa	se	ga	takai	desu.
	kami		nagai	
	me		ōkii	

4.

Ano hito wa			
		wakakute,	kirei desu.
	atama ga	yokute,	hansamu desu.
		kirei de,	taihen shinsetsu desu.

Renshū B

1. Rei : nichi-yōbi Nagoya e ikimasu, tomodachi ni aimasu
   ······Nichi-yōbi Nagoya e itte, tomodachi ni aimasu.
   1) heya e kaerimasu, yasumimasu ······
   2) gogo kōjō o kengaku-shimasu, 6-ji goro Sentā e kaerimasu ······
   3) Shinjuku made densha de ikimasu, chikatetsu ni norikaemasu ······
   4) Tōkyō-eki de densha ni norimasu, Yokohama-eki de orite kudasai ······

2. Rei : ······ 6-ji ni okite, gohan o tabete, sorekara kaisha e ikimasu.
   1) ······
   2) ······

3. Rei : 5-shūkan Nihon-go o benkyō-shimasu, jisshū ni ikimasu
   ······5-shūkan Nihon-go o benkyō-shite kara, jisshū ni ikimasu.
   1) kuni e kaerimasu, sugu kekkon-shimasu ······
   2) kōgi ga owarimasu, tenisu o shimasen ka ······
   3) densha o orimasu, uchi made 10-pun gurai arukimasu ······
   4) kinō kazoku ni tegami o kakimashita, nemashita ······

4. Rei :   Bangohan o tabete kara, nani o shimasu ka.

    ······Benkyō-shite, terebi o mimasu.

    1) Kōgi ga owatte kara, nani o shimasu ka. ······

    2) Shigoto ga owatte kara, nani o shimasu ka. ······

    3) Uchi e kaette kara, nani o shimasu ka. ······

5. Rei 1 : Fujisan wa takai desu,   kirei desu

    ······Fujisan wa takakute, kirei desu.

    Rei 2 : Sāto-san wa kirei desu,   shinsetsu desu

    ······Sāto-san wa kirei de, shinsetsu desu.

    1) Rao-san no rajikase wa chiisai desu,   karui desu ······

    2) Shinjuku wa nigiyaka desu,   omoshiroi machi desu ······

    3) Narong-san wa Tai-jin desu,   Nagoya-jidōsha no kenshūsei desu ······

    4) watashi no heya wa hiroi desu,   akarui desu ······

6. Rei :   Kimura-san wa donna hito desu ka. (wakai, kireina hito)

    ······Wakakute, kireina hito desu.

    1) Ano resutoran wa dō desu ka. (oishii, yasui) ······

    2) Anata no machi wa donna machi desu ka. (shizuka, kireina machi) ······

    3) Han-san wa donna hito desu ka. (atama ga ii, shinsetsuna hito) ······

    4) Kinō no pātii wa dō deshita ka. (hito ga ōi, tanoshii) ······

Renshū C

1. A : Kinō Tōkyō e ikimashita.

    B : Sō desu ka.   Tōkyō e itte, nani o shimashita ka.

    A : Tomodachi ni atte, <u>eiga o mite</u>, sorekara
    ① issho ni <u>biiru o nomimashita.</u>
    ②

    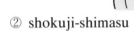
    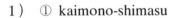

    1)   ① kaimono-shimasu   ② shokuji-shimasu
    2)   ① kōen o sanpo-shimasu   ② eiga o mimasu
    3)   ① iroiro hanashimasu   ② kaimono ni ikimasu

2. A : Eiga o mi ni ikimasen ka.

    B : Ii desu ne.   Nan-ji goro ikimasu ka.

    A : <u>Hirugohan o tabete</u> kara, sugu ikimashō.

    1)   kōgi ga owarimasu
    2)   shokuji-shimasu
    3)   shigoto ga owarimasu

3. A : Ano hito wa dare desu ka.

    B : Dono hito desu ka.

    A : Ano <u>wakakute,</u> kireina hito desu.

    B : Ā, ano hito wa Han-san desu.

    1)   kami ga nagai desu
    2)   se ga takai desu
    3)   dansu ga jōzu desu

Mondai

1. 1) _____

   2) _____

   3) _____

   4) _____

   5) _____

2.

1) Futari wa ⎰ a. ima sugu ⎱ (   ) o shimasu.

   { a. ima sugu
     b. ato de mata
     c. hirugohan o tabete kara }

2) Rao-san wa Shinjuku de
   { a. machi o kenbutsu-shite, eiga o mite,
     b. kaimono-shite, eiga o mite,
     c. shokuji-shite, kaimono-shite, }

   (   ) o tabemashita.

3) Koko kara Nagoya-kōen made
   { a. chikatetsu
     b. basu
     c. chikatetsu to basu }
   de ikimasu.

   (   ) gurai kakarimasu.

4) Ōsaka wa
   { a. omoshirokute,
     b. ōkikute,
     c. hito ga ōkute, }
   (   ) de, nigiyakana machi desu.

5) Satō-san wa
   { a. se ga takakute,
     b. kami ga nagakute,
     c. taihen wakakute, }
   (   ) ga jōzu desu.

3. Rei : Mō sukoshi yukkuri (arukimasu ⋯ aruite) kudasai.

1) Koko de te o (araimasu ⋯ あらって) kudasai.

2) Kengaku ni ikimasu kara, hayaku basu ni (norimasu ⋯ のって) kudasai.

3) Densha o (orimasu ⋯ おりて) kara, Sentā made 10-pun gurai arukimasu.

4) Shawā o (abimasu ⋯ あびて) kara, bangohan o tabemasu.

5) Bangohan o tabete kara, shinbun o (yomimasu ⋯ よんで), kazoku ni tegami o (kakimasu ⋯ かいて), sorekara nemashita.

6) Nara wa (shizuka desu ⋯ しずかで), kireina machi desu.

7) Rao-san wa atama ga (ii desu ⋯ よくて), hansamuna hito desu.

8) Kono mise wa hanbāgu ga (oishii desu ⋯ おいしくて), yasui desu.

9) (Chiisai desu ⋯ ちいさくて), karui tēpu-rekōdā ga hoshii desu.

4. Watashi wa maiasa 7-ji goro okite, asagohan o tabete, kaisha e ikimasu. Watashi no kaisha wa konpyūta no kaisha de, Tōkyō ni arimasu. Uchi kara kaisha made 1-jikan han gurai kakarimasu. Maiasa eki made basu de itte, soko de densha ni norikaete, Tōkyō made ikimasu. Shigoto wa 9-ji kara 5-ji made desu. Do-yōbi wa yasumi desu. Kin-yōbi no yoru shigoto ga owatte kara, itsumo tomodachi to shokuji ni ikimasu. Konshū wa shigoto ga takusan arimashita kara, tsukaremashita. Kyō sugu uchi e kaette, yasumimasu.

Rei : Watashi wa maiasa 6-ji goro okimasu. (×)

Watashi wa maiasa 7-ji goro okimasu. (○)

1) Maiasa asagohan o tabete kara, kaisha e ikimasu. (○)

2) Kaisha wa Tōkyō ni atte, uchi kara tōi desu. (○)

3) Eki made aruite, densha de kaisha e ikimasu. (×)

4) Konshū wa taihen isogashikatta desu. (○)

5) Kyō shigoto ga owatte kara, tomodachi to shokuji ni ikimasu. (×)

Dai 17 ka

Bunkei

1. Shashin o toranai de kudasai.

2. Mainichi benkyō-shinakereba narimasen.
   (benkyō-shinai to ikemasen)

3. Do-yōbi no gogo benkyō-shinakute mo ii desu.

Reibun

1. Abunai desu kara, kono kikai ni sawaranai de kudasai.
   ···Wakarimashita. Ki o tsukemasu.

2. Kōhii ni satō o iremashō ka.
   ···Iie, irenai de kudasai.

3. Kōjō no hito wa Eigo ga wakarimasu ka.
   ···Iie, wakarimasen.
   Desukara, Nihon-go de hanasanakereba narimasen.

4. Nan-ji made ni Sentā e kaeranakereba narimasen ka.
   ···12-ji made ni kaeranakereba narimasen.

5. Mainichi repōto o dasanakereba narimasen ka.
   ···Iie, mainichi dasanakute mo ii desu.
   Maishū kin-yōbi ni dashite kudasai.

Kaiwa

Kōjō-kengaku

Tanaka : Kōjō no naka de kikai ya seihin ni sawaranai de
kudasai.

Rao : Wakarimashita.

Rao : Wā, sugoi oto desu ne.

Tanaka-san, ano robotto no shashin o totte mo
ii desu ka.

Tanaka : Iie, dame desu.

Kyoka o morawanakereba narimasen.

Rao : Sō desu ka. Zannen desu.

Renshū A

1.

masu-kei			nai-kei		
I	i	ki masu	i	ka	nai
	iso	gi masu	iso	ga	nai
	no	mi masu	no	ma	nai
	yo	bi masu	yo	ba	nai
	kae	ri masu	kae	ra	nai
	su	i masu	su	wa	nai
	ma	chi masu	ma	ta	nai
	hana	shi masu	hana	sa	nai

masu-kei		nai-kei	
II	tabe masu	tabe	nai
	ire masu	ire	nai
	oki masu	oki	nai
	kari masu	kari	nai
	ori masu	ori	nai
	abi masu	abi	nai
	mi masu	mi	nai
	i masu	i	nai

masu-kei		nai-kei	
III	ki masu		ko nai
	shi masu		shi nai
	shinpai- shi masu	shinpai-	shi nai

2.

Suitchi ni	sawara	nai de kudasai.
Pasupōto o	nakusa	
Kūrā o	tsuke	

3.

Repōto o	kaka	nakereba narimasen.
Nihon-go o	benkyō-shi	
Kutsu o	nuga	

4.

Namae o	kaka	nakute mo ii desu.
Okane o	harawa	
Pasupōto o	mise	

17

Renshū B

1. Rei : kono taipu o tsukaimasu ······Kono taipu o tsukawanai de kudasai.

   1) denwa-bangō o wasuremasu ······

   2) koko de tabako o suimasu ······

   3) koko ni kuruma o tomemasu ······

   4) kōjō no naka de shashin o torimasu ······

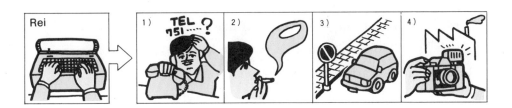

2. Rei : kin'en desu, tabako o suimasu

   ······Kin'en desu kara, tabako o suwanai de kudasai.

   1) samui desu, mado o akemasu ······

   2) watashi wa genki desu, shinpai-shimasu ······

   3) kore wa taisetsuna hon desu, nakushimasu ······

   4) abunai desu, kikai ni sawarimasu ······

3. Rei : hayaku uchi e kaerimasu

   ······Hayaku uchi e kaeranakereba narimasen.

   1) kusuri o nomimasu ······

   2) kaisha ni denwa o kakemasu ······

   3) mainichi 3-jikan benkyō-shimasu ······

   4) maiasa hayaku okimasu ······

4. Rei : Sentā e nan-ji made ni kaeranakereba narimasen ka. (12-ji)

   ······12-ji made ni kaeranakereba narimasen.

   1) Nan-mai repōto o kakanakereba narimasen ka. (5-mai) ······

   2) Itsu made ni kono hon o kaesanakereba narimasen ka. (do-yōbi) ······

   3) Nihon de donokurai jisshū-shinakereba narimasen ka. (6-kagetsu) ······

   4) Nan-ji made ni kyōshitsu e konakereba narimasen ka. (9-ji) ······

5. Rei : pasupōto o misemasu ······Pasupōto o misenakute mo ii desu.

    1) hon o kaeshimasu ······

    2) mainichi repōto o dashimasu ······

    3) do-yōbi hatarakimasu ······

    4) kaisha ni denwa o kakemasu ······

6. Rei 1 : mō 11-ji desu, Sentā e kaerimasu

            ······Mō 11-ji desu kara, Sentā e kaeranakereba narimasen.

    Rei 2 : jikan ga arimasu, isogimasen

            ······Jikan ga arimasu kara, isoganakute mo ii desu.

    1) uchi wa eki kara tōi desu, 20-pun gurai arukimasu ······

    2) ashita wa yasumi desu, benkyō-shimasen ······

    3) kōjō no hito wa Eigo ga wakarimasen, Nihon-go de hanashimasu ······

    4) netsu ga arimasen, byōin e ikimasen ······

7. Rei : Kono hon o yomanakereba narimasen ka. (iie)

           ······Iie, yomanakute mo ii desu.

    1) Maiban tēpu o kikanakereba narimasen ka. (hai) ······

    2) Kōjō e itte kara, Nihon-go de hanasanakereba narimasen ka. (hai) ······

    3) Sentā de kutsu o nuganakereba narimasen ka. (iie) ······

    4) Kono jisho o kaesanakereba narimasen ka. (iie) ······

Renshū C

1. A : Abunai desu kara, <u>koko de tabako o suwanai</u> de kudasai.

   B : Hai, wakarimashita.   Ki o tsukemasu.

   1） koko ni hairimasu
   2） sochira e ikimasu
   3） kikai ni sawarimasu

2. A : Issho ni shokuji ni ikimasen ka.

   B : Sumimasen.
   Korekara <u>byōin e ika</u>nakereba narimasen kara.

   1） repōto o kakimasu
   2） kaisha no hito ni aimasu
   3） shukudai o shimasu

3. A : <u>Takushii o yobimashō</u> ka.
   ①
   B : Iie, <u>yobanakute</u> mo ii desu.
   ①
   <u>Aruite ikimasu</u> kara.
   ②

   1） ① kūrā o tsukemasu
      ② atsukunai desu
   2） ① Eigo de hanashimasu
      ② Nihon-go ga wakarimasu
   3） ① mō sukoshi satō o iremasu
      ② amai desu

Mondai

1. 1) _____
    2) _____
    3) _____
    4) _____
    5) _____

2.

1) Kono kagi wa (   ) desu kara, { a. nakusa / b. kaesa / c. dasa } nai de kudasai.

2) Konban { a. depāto e ikanakereba narimasen / b. kaisha no hito ni awanakereba narimasen / c. repōto o kakanakereba narimasen } kara,
   asobi ni (   ).

3) (   ) o kaesanakereba narimasen.
   Demo, tēpu o { a. kaesanakereba narimasen. / b. kaesanakute mo ii desu. / c. kikanakereba narimasen. }

4) Kyō wa (   ) desu kara, kūrā o { a. tsukete kudasai. / b. tsukete mo ii desu. / c. tsukenakute mo ii desu. }

5) (   ) made ni, denwa no okane o { a. hairanakereba narimasen. / b. harawanakereba narimasen. / c. harawanakute mo ii desu. }

3.

Rei : ikimasu	ikanai	iimasu		(6-ji ni) okimasu	
kikimasu		asobimasu		mimasu	
hanashimasu		nugimasu		shimasu	
hairimasu		akemasu		jisshū-shimasu	
tsukaimasu		iremasu		(Nihon e) kimasu	

4. Rei : Hiitā o (keshimasu … kesa) nai de kudasai.

1) Shukudai o (wasuremasu …　　　　　　) nai de kudasai.

2) Koko ni kuruma o (tomemasu …　　　　　　) nai de kudasai.

3) Koko de tabako o (suimasu …　　　　　) nai de kudasai.

4) Abunai desu kara, suitchi ni (sawarimasu …　　　　　) nai de kudasai.

5) Ashita made ni kono kikai o (shūri-shimasu …　　　　) nakereba narimasen.

6) Netsu ga arimasu kara, sugu byōin e (ikimasu …　　　　) nakereba narimasen.

7) Jikan ga arimasu kara, (isogimasu …　　　　) nakute mo ii desu.

8) Aruite ikimasu kara, takushii o (yobimasu …　　　　) nakute mo ii desu.

5.

| Katō-san, o-genki desu ka.　Mainichi samui desu ga, watashi wa genki desu kara, shinpai-shinai de kudasai.　Nihon e kite kara, mō 3-shūkan desu. Nihon-go no benkyō wa omoshiroi desu ga, sukoshi muzukashii desu. Itsumo Sentā no hito to Nihon-go de hanashimasu ga, tokidoki kotoba o wasuremasu.　Kōjō e itte kara, Nihon-go de hanasanakereba narimasen. Desukara, chotto shinpai desu.　Ashita wa yasumi desu kara, benkyō ga arimasen.　Desukara, konban hayaku nemasu.　Mata tegami o kakimasu. Karada ni ki o tsukete kudasai.　Sayōnara　　　　　　　　　　Rao |

Rei : Rao-san wa Katō-san ni tegami o kakimashita.　　(○)

Katō-san wa Rao-san ni tegami o kakimashita.　　(✕)

1) Rao-san wa ima kōjō de jisshū-shite imasu.　　(　　)

2) Rao-san wa genki desu kara, Katō-san wa shinpai-shinakute mo ii desu.　(　)

3) Rao-san wa Sentā no hito to tokidoki Nihon-go de hanashimasu.　(　　)

4) Kōjō no hito wa Eigo ga jōzu desu kara, Rao-san wa Nihon-go de hanasanakute mo ii desu.　(　)

5) Ashita Nihon-go o benkyō-shinakute mo ii desu.　　(　　)

Dai 18 ka

Bunkei

1. Lee-san wa kanji o yomu koto ga dekimasu.
2. Watashi no shumi wa eiga o miru koto desu.
3. Neru mae ni, hon o yomimasu.

Reibun

1. Sukii ga dekimasu ka.

   ···Hai, dekimasu.   Demo, amari jōzu dewa arimasen.

2. Gitā o hiku koto ga dekimasu ka.

   ···Iie, dekimasen.

3. Uketsuke de doru o en ni kaeru koto ga dekimasu ka.

   ···Iie, dekimasen.   Ginkō e itte kudasai.

4. Shumi wa nan desu ka.

   ···Ongaku o kiku koto desu.

5. Nihon e kuru mae ni, Nihon-go o benkyō-shimashita ka.

   ···Iie, zenzen shimasendeshita.   Nihon e kite kara,

   hajimemashita.

6. Kōgi no mae ni, chotto jimusho e kite kudasai.

   ···Hai, wakarimashita.

7. Itsu kekkon-shimashita ka.

   ···3-nen mae ni kekkon-shimashita.

Kaiwa

Sukii

Kimura : Raishū sukii ni ikimasen ka.

Rao : Ikitai desu ga, watashi wa sukii ga dekimasen.

Kimura : Daijōbu desu yo. Kantan desu kara.

Rao : Kimura-san wa sukii ga jōzu desu ne.

Kimura : Rao-san mo jōzu desu yo.

Rao : Iie, mada mada dame desu.

Motto renshū-shinai to···.

Kimura : Ja, hirugohan o taberu mae ni, mō sukoshi
renshū-shimashō.

Renshū A

1.

masu-kei			jisho-kei	
I	ka	ki masu	ka	ku
	iso	gi masu	iso	gu
	yasu	mi masu	yasu	mu
	yo	bi masu	yo	bu
	to	ri masu	to	ru
	ka	i masu	ka	u
	ma	chi masu	ma	tsu
	hana	shi masu	hana	su

masu-kei			jisho-kei	
II	tabe	masu	tabe	ru
	ne	masu	ne	ru
	mi	masu	mi	ru
	oki	masu	oki	ru
	kari	masu	kari	ru

masu-kei			jisho-kei	
III		ki masu		kuru
		shi masu		suru
	benkyō-	shi masu	benkyō-	suru
	unten-	shi masu	unten-	suru

2. Watashi wa | tenisu | ga dekimasu.
   | Nihon-go |
   | jidōsha no unten |

3. Ano hito wa | Nihon-go o | hanasu | koto ga dekimasu.
   | piano o | hiku |
   | kanji o | yomu |

4. Watashi no shumi wa | | oyogu | koto desu.
   | shashin o | toru |
   | e o | kaku |

5. | Gohan o | taberu | mae ni, | te o araimasu.
   | | Neru | | shawā o abimasu.
   | Nihon e | kuru | | Nihon-go o benkyō-shimashita.

Renshū B

1. Rei :　……Anata wa tenisu ga dekimasu ka.
   👉 1)　……
   　　2)　……
   　　3)　……
   　　4)　……

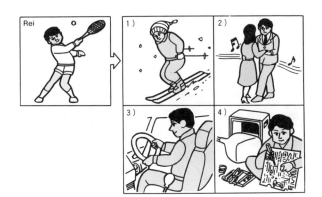

2. Rei :　hiragana o kakimasu ……Hiragana o kaku koto ga dekimasu.
   1)　kanji o yomimasu ……
   2)　Nihon-go o hanashimasu ……
   3)　Nihon no uta o utaimasu ……
   4)　Nihon-go de denwa o kakemasu ……

3. Rei :　Hashi de gohan o taberu koto ga dekimasu ka. (iie)
   　　　　……Iie, dekimasen.
   1)　Nihon-go de tegami o kaku koto ga dekimasu ka. (iie) ……
   2)　Terebi no koshō o naosu koto ga dekimasu ka. (hai) ……
   3)　Uketsuke de takushii o yobu koto ga dekimasu ka. (hai) ……
   4)　Heya kara kuni ni denwa o kakeru koto ga dekimasu ka. (iie) ……

4. Rei : Shumi wa nan desu ka. ······Hon o yomu koto desu.

   1) Shumi wa nan desu ka. ······

   2) Shumi wa nan desu ka. ······

   3) Shumi wa nan desu ka. ······

   4) Shumi wa nan desu ka. ······

5. Rei : nemasu, shawā o abimasu ······Neru mae ni, shawā o abimasu.

   1) kuni e kaerimasu, omiyage o kaimasu ······

   2) ryokō ni ikimasu, kasa o kaimasu ······

   3) gohan o tabemasu, te o araimasu ······

   4) Nihon e kimashita, sukoshi Nihon-go o benkyō-shimashita ······

6. Rei : Bangohan no mae ni, nani o shimasu ka. (tenisu)

       ······Tenisu o shimasu.

   1) Kuni e kaeru mae ni, nani o kaitai desu ka. (sutereo) ······

   2) Nihon e kuru mae ni, donokurai Nihon-go o benkyō-shimashita ka.

       (3-kagetsu) ······

   3) Jisshū no mae ni, donokurai Nihon-go o naraimasu ka.

       (5-shūkan) ······

   4) Itsu Nihon e kimashita ka. (2-kagetsu mae ni) ······

Renshū C

1. A : <u>Kanji o yomu</u> koto ga dekimasu ka.
      ①
   B : Ē, dekimasu.
   A : Ja, sumimasen ga, kono <u>tegami</u> o
                              ②
      <u>yonde</u> kudasai.
      ①
   B : Ii desu yo.

   1) ① rajio o naoshimasu   ② rajio
   2) ① gitā o hikimasu   ② uta
   3) ① tokei o shūri-shimasu   ② tokei

2. A : Shumi wa nan desu ka.
   B : <u>Eiga o miru</u> koto desu.
   A : Sō desu ka.   Watashi mo desu.
      Ja, nichi-yōbi issho ni <u>eiga o mi</u> ni
      ikimashō.

   1) oyogimasu
   2) shashin o torimasu
   3) e o kakimasu

3. A : <u>Watashi no uchi e kuru</u> mae ni, <u>denwa o kakete</u> kudasai.
      ①   ②
   B : Hai, wakarimashita.

   1) ① nemasu   ② denki o keshimasu
   2) ① shukudai o shimasu ② nōto o yoku mimasu
   3) ① gohan o tabemasu   ② kusuri o nomimasu

Mondai

1. 1) _____
    🔊 2) _____
    3) _____
    4) _____
    5) _____

2. 1) Kimura-san wa (   ) mae ni kuruma no unten o

    🔊 naraimashita kara, { a. unten ga jōzu desu. / b. unten ga dekimasu. / c. unten ga dekimasen. }

    2) Lee-san wa tegami no jūsho o (   ) de { a. kaku / b. yomu / c. oshieru } koto ga

    dekimasu.

    3) Yūbinkyoku de (   ) o { a. oku / b. kaeru / c. okuru } koto ga dekimasu.

    4) Narong-san wa { a. Nihon e kuru mae ni, / b. Nihon e kite kara, / c. kuni e kaette kara, } (   ) no benkyō o

    hajimemashita.

    5) Lee-san no shumi wa (   ) koto desu. { a. Maiasa 1-jikan / b. Maiban 1-jikan / c. Mainichi 2-jikan }

    gurai yomimasu.

3.

Rei : ikimasu	iku	hairimasu		(6-ji ni) okimasu	
kikimasu		aimasu		abimasu	
dashimasu		isogimasu		mimasu	
machimasu		asobimasu		shimasu	
yomimasu		kakemasu		(Nihon e) kimasu	

4. Rei : (Jisshū-shimasu …Jisshū-suru) mae ni, Nihon-go o naraimasu.

1) Watashi no shumi wa e o (kakimasu …   ) koto desu.

2) Uketsuke de takushii o (yobimasu …   ) koto ga dekimasu.

3) Kuni e (kaerimasu …   ) mae ni, iroirona omiyage o kaimasu.

4) Uchi e (kaerimasu …   ) kara, bangohan o tabemasu.

5) Gohan o (tabemasu …   ) mae ni, yoku te o aratte kudasai.

6) Watashi wa 500-mētoru gurai (oyogimasu …   ) koto ga dekimasu.

7) Kuruma no unten ga dekimasu ga, koshō o (naoshimasu …   )
     koto ga dekimasen.

8) Piano o (hikimasu …   ) koto ga dekimasen.

5. Watashi no shumi wa kuruma no unten desu.   5-nen mae ni jidōsha-gakkō e
itte, unten o naraimashita.   Nihon de 18-sai kara kuruma no unten
ga dekimasu.   Nihon wa kuruma ga ōi desu kara, abunai desu.   Desukara,
unten ni ki o tsukenakereba narimasen.   Watashi wa tokidoki kazoku to
issho ni kuruma de iroirona tokoro e asobi ni ikimasu.

Sengetsu kuruma de sukii ni ikimashita.   Kanai wa unten ga dekimasen.
Demo, watashi wa unten ga suki desu kara, zenzen tsukaremasendeshita.   Ima
atarashii kuruma ga hoshii desu ga, takai desu kara, kau koto ga dekimasen.
Zannen desu.

Rei : Watashi no shumi wa kuruma no unten desu.   (○)

Watashi no shumi wa kuruma no shūri desu.   (✕)

1) Watashi wa 5-nen mae ni hitori de kuruma no unten o
     benkyō-shimashita.   (   )

2) Nihon de 18-sai kara kuruma o unten-shite mo ii desu.   (   )

3) 3-kagetsu mae ni kazoku to kuruma de sukii ni ikimashita.   (   )

4) Kanai wa kuruma no unten ga dekimasen.   (   )

5) Raigetsu atarashii kuruma o kaimasu.   (   )

Dai 19 ka

Bunkei

1. Nihon-ryōri o tabeta koto ga arimasu.

2. Nichi-yōbi kaimono-shitari, eiga o mitari shimasu.

3. Korekara dandan samuku narimasu.

Reibun

1. Indoneshia e itta koto ga arimasu ka.

   ···Hai, arimasu.   3-nen mae ni tomodachi to ikimashita.

2. Fujisan o mita koto ga arimasu ka.

   ···Iie, ichido mo arimasen.   Zehi mitai desu.

3. Sentā de mainichi nani o shimasu ka.

   ···Nihon-go o benkyō-shitari, kōgi o kiitari shimasu.

4. Nichi-yōbi dokoka dekakemashita ka.

   ···Iie.   Uchi de hon o yondari, tegami o kaitari shimashita.

5. Kuraku narimashita ne.   Denki o tsukemashō ka.

   ···Ē, onegai-shimasu.

6. Otōsan no byōki wa dō desu ka.

   ···Mō genki ni narimashita.

Kaiwa

Hōmon

Narong	:	Gomen kudasai.
Yamamoto	:	Yā, irasshai. Sā, dōzo.
Narong	:	Shitsurei-shimasu.

Okusan	:	Sukiyaki desu. Tabeta koto ga arimasu ka.
Narong	:	Iie, arimasen. Hajimete desu.
Okusan	:	Sō desu ka. Oishii desu yo.
		Dōzo takusan tabete kudasai.

153

Narong	:	Mō 9-ji desu ne.
		Sorosoro shitsurei-shimasu.
		Kyō wa dōmo arigatō gozaimashita.

Renshū A

1.

	masu-kei			ta-kei		
I	ka	ki	masu	ka	i	ta
	*i	ki	masu	i	t	ta
	iso	gi	masu	iso	i	da
	no	mi	masu	no	n	da
	yo	bi	masu	yo	n	da
	to	ri	masu	to	t	ta
	ka	i	masu	ka	t	ta
	ma	chi	masu	ma	t	ta
	ka	shi	masu	ka	shi	ta

	masu-kei		ta-kei	
II	tabe	masu	tabe	ta
	dekake	masu	dekake	ta
	oki	masu	oki	ta
	abi	masu	abi	ta
	deki	masu	deki	ta
	mi	masu	mi	ta

	masu-kei		ta-kei	
III	ki	masu	ki	ta
	shi	masu	shi	ta
	shūri-shi	masu	shūri-shi	ta

2. Watashi wa

Fujisan o	mita	koto ga arimasu.
tenpura o	tabeta	
shinkansen ni	notta	

3. Yoru

terebi o	mita	ri,	tomodachi to	hanashita	ri shimasu.
ongaku o	kiita		hon o	yonda	
shukudai o	shita		tegami o	kaita	

4.

Dandan atsu	ku	narimasu.
Nihon-go ga jōzu	ni	
Raigetsu 25-sai	ni	

Renshū B

1. Rei : ⋯⋯Sakura o mita koto ga arimasu.
 1) ⋯⋯
   2) ⋯⋯
   3) ⋯⋯
   4) ⋯⋯
   5) ⋯⋯

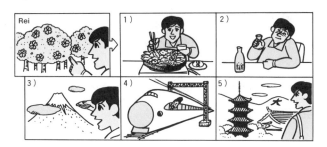

2. Rei : Yuki o mita koto ga arimasu ka. (iie) ⋯⋯Iie, arimasen.
   1) Sushi o tabeta koto ga arimasu ka. (hai) ⋯⋯
   2) Nihon-jin no uchi ni tomatta koto ga arimasu ka. (iie, ichido mo) ⋯⋯
   3) Gaikoku e itta koto ga arimasu ka. (hai) ⋯⋯
   4) Shinkansen no naka de shokuji-shita koto ga arimasu ka.
      (iie, ichido mo) ⋯⋯

3. Rei : yoru ⋯⋯ Yoru hon o yondari, ongaku o kiitari shimasu.
 1) nichi-yōbi ⋯⋯
   2) gogo ⋯⋯
   3) nichi-yōbi ⋯⋯
   4) kinō ⋯⋯

4. Rei : Kinō nani o shimashita ka. (terebi o mimashita,　pinpon o shimashita)
　　　　······Terebi o mitari, pinpon o shitari shimashita.
　1） Yoru itsumo nani o shimasu ka.
　　　(tomodachi to hanashimasu,　tegami o kakimasu) ······
　2） Kinō nani o shimashita ka.
　　　(depāto de kaimono-shimashita,　machi o kenbutsu-shimashita) ······
　3） Nichi-yōbi itsumo nani o shimasu ka.
　　　(tenisu o shimasu,　tomodachi no uchi e asobi ni ikimasu) ······
　4） Nihon de nani o shinakereba narimasen ka.
　　　(Nihon-go o benkyō-shinakereba narimasen,　kōjō de
　　　jisshū-shinakereba narimasen) ······

5. Rei 1 : kami ga nagai desu ······Kami ga nagaku narimashita.
　Rei 2 : Rao-san wa genki desu ······Rao-san wa genki ni narimashita.
　1） soto wa kurai desu ······
　2） atama ga itai desu ······
　3） Narong-san wa Nihon-go ga jōzu desu ······
　4） watashi wa Nihon-ryōri ga suki desu ······
　5） kodomo wa se ga takai desu ······
　6） Ali-san wa byōki desu ······

Renshū C

1. A : <u>Ginza e itta</u> koto ga arimasu ka.
        ①
    B : Ē, arimasu. Sengetsu <u>ikimashita</u>.
                           ①
    A : Dō deshita ka.
    B : Totemo <u>nigiyaka deshita.</u>
                 ②

    1) ① tenpura o tabemasu   ② oishii desu
    2) ① shinkansen ni norimasu   ② hayai desu
    3) ① kabuki o mimasu   ② kirei desu

2. A : Nichi-yōbi dokoka ikimashita ka.
    B : Iie, doko mo ikimasendeshita.
        Uchi de <u>sentaku-shitari</u>, <u>sōji-shitari</u> shimashita.
                  ①   ②

    1) ① benkyō-shimasu
         ② repōto o kakimasu
    2) ① ongaku o kikimasu
         ② zasshi o yomimasu
    3) ① kodomo to asobimasu
         ② terebi o mimasu

3. A : <u>Atsuku</u> narimashita ne.
        ①
    B : Sō desu ne. <u>Mado o akemashō ka.</u>
                     ②
    A : Ē, onegai-shimasu.

    1) ① samui desu   ② mado o shimemasu
    2) ① kurai desu   ② denki o tsukemasu
    3) ① atsui desu   ② kūrā o tsukemasu

Mondai

1. 1) _____
   2) _____
   3) _____
   4) _____
   5) _____

2.
1) Kimura-san wa
   { a. 1-nen Tai ni ita
     b. 1-nen mae ni Tai e itta } koto ga arimasu.
     c. 2-kai Tai-ryōri o tabeta }

   Tai wa totemo (   ).

2) Han-san wa
   { a. kabuki o mita
     b. kippu o katta } koto ga arimasen kara,
     c. kabuki o shita }

   kabuki o mi ni (   ).

3) Katō-san wa nichi-yōbi (   ) to
   { a. machi o kenbutsu-shitari,
     b. kōen o sanpo-shitari,   } depāto de kaimono-shitari shimasu.
     c. resutoran de shokuji-shitari, }

4) Kinō doko mo (   ).
   { a. Hon o yondari, terebi o mitari
     b. Hon o yondari, rajio o kiitari }
     c. Tegami o kaitari, hon o yondari }

   shimashita.

5) (   ) narimashita kara,
   { a. kūrā o tsukete kudasai.
     b. denki o tsukete kudasai. }
     c. hiitā o tsukete kudasai. }

3.

Rei : ikimasu	itta	kaimasu		dekakemasu	
kakimasu		asobimasu		abimasu	
norimasu		oyogimasu		shokuji-shimasu	
hanashimasu		nemasu		(Nihon e) kimasu	

4. Rei : Sashimi o (tabemasu ··· tabeta) koto ga arimasu.

 1) Nihon-jin no uchi ni (tomarimasu ···   ) koto ga arimasu.

 2) Katō-san no okusan ni (aimasu ···   ) koto ga arimasu.

 3) Ichido mo Nihon no eiga o (mimasu ···   ) koto ga arimasen.

 4) Tanaka-san no uchi de sukiyaki o (tabemasu ···   ) ri, o-sake o
    (nomimasu ···   ) ri shimashita.

 5) Nichi-yōbi (sōji-shimasu ···   ) ri,
    (sentaku-shimasu ···   ) ri shinakereba narimasen.

5. Rei : (Atsui desu ··· Atsuku) narimashita kara, (b   )

 1) (Kurai desu ···   ) narimashita kara, (   )

 2) (Genki desu ···   ) narimashita kara, (   )

 3) Kami ga (nagai desu ···   ) narimashita kara, (   )

 4) Ii (tenki desu ···   ) narimashita kara, (   )

 5) (9-ji desu ···   ) narimashita kara, (   )

 a. kōen e asobi ni ikimasu.

 b. mado o akemasu.

 c. kiritai desu.

 d. kyōshitsu e ikanakereba narimasen.

 e. byōin e ikanakute mo ii desu.

 f. denki o tsukemasu.

6.

> Watashi wa mainichi Sentā de Nihon-go o (benkyō-shimasu ···
> benkyō-shita) ri, kōgi o (kikimasu ···   ) ri shimasu. Gogo tokidoki
> kōjō e (kengaku-shimasu ···   ) ni ikimasu. Sentā no benkyō ga
> (owarimasu ···   ) kara, ryokō ni ikimasu. Soshite kōjō o
> (kengaku-shimasu ···   ) ri, Nihon no yūmeina tokoro o
> (kenbutsu-shimasu ···   ) ri shimasu.
>
> Watashi wa ichido mo Kyōto ya Nara e (ikimasu ···   ) koto ga
> arimasen. Desukara, hayaku (ikimasu ···   ) tai desu. Soshite
> Shinkansen ni zehi (norimasu ···   ) tai desu.

Fukushū C

1.

Rei : kakimasu	kaite	kakanai	kaku	kaita
kikimasu				
nugimasu				
ikimasu				
nomimasu				
yobimasu				
torimasu				
suimasu				
tachimasu				
kashimasu				
kaemasu				
iremasu				
(6-ji ni) okimasu				
mimasu				
karimasu				
imasu				
abimasu				
orimasu				
dekimasu				
(Nihon e) kimasu				
shimasu				
unten-shimasu				

2. Rei : Watashi (wa) Rao desu.

1) Ame (   ) futte imasu ne. Kasa (   ) arimasu ka.

2) Kasa (   ) motte imasu.

3) Kono kanji (   ) yomi-kata (   ) oshiete kudasai.

4) Koko (   ) suwatte mo ii desu ka.

5) Eki no mae de basu (   ) notte, Kōen-mae de basu
(   ) orimasu.

6) Abunai desu kara, kono kikai (   ) sawaranai de kudasai.

7) Karada (   ) ki o tsukete kudasai.

8) Kuruma (   ) unten (   ) dekimasu.

3. Rei : Chotto (machimasu ··· matte   ) kudasai.

   1) Issho ni ocha o (nomimasu ···   ) masen ka.

   2) 3-ji ni eki de (aimasu ···   ) mashō.

   3) Tsukaremashita kara, sukoshi (yasumimasu ···   ) tai desu.

   4) Depāto e kutsu o (kaimasu ···   ) ni ikimasu.

   5) Sumimasen ga, takushii o (yobimasu ···   ) kudasai.

   6) Ima tegami o (kakimasu ···   ) imasu.

   7) Koko de tabako o (suimasu ···   ) mo ii desu ka.

   8) Sentā no jūsho o (shirimasu ···   ) imasu.

   9) Bangohan o (tabemasu ···   ), (benkyō-shimasu ···   ),
      sorekara nemasu.

   10) Kimura-san wa (kirei desu ···   ), shinsetsuna hito desu.

   11) Rao-san wa se ga (takai desu ···   ), hansamu desu.

   12) Shawā o (abimasu ···   ) kara, nemasu.

   13) Abunai desu kara, koko ni (hairimasu ···   ) nai de kudasai.

   14) Kaisha ni repōto o (kakimasu ···   ) nakereba narimasen.

   15) Nichi-yōbi (hatarakimasu ···   ) nakute mo ii desu.

   16) Nihon-go o (hanashimasu ···   ) koto ga dekimasu.

   17) Shumi wa ongaku o (kikimasu ···   ) koto desu.

   18) Nihon e (kimasu ···   ) mae ni, sukoshi Nihon-go o
      benkyō-shimashita.

   19) Kyōto e (ikimasu ···   ) koto ga arimasu ka.

   20) Nichi-yōbi itsumo terebi o (mimasu ···   ) ri, hon o
      (yomimasu ···   ) ri shimasu.

   21) (Kurai desu ···   ) narimashita kara, denki o
      (tsukemasu ···   ) kudasai.

   22) Nihon-go ga (jōzu desu ···   ) narimashita.

C

Dai 20 ka

Bunkei

1. Ashita Tōkyō e iku.
2. Mainichi isogashii.
3. Kyō wa ii tenki da.

Reibun

1. Kōhii o nomu?

   ···Un, nomu.

   ···Uun, nomanai.

2. Heya ni terebi ga aru?

   ···Uun, nai.

3. Depāto de nani o katta?

   ···Nani mo kawanakatta.

4. Issho ni gohan o tabenai?

   ···Un, ii ne.

5. Nihon no tabemono wa dō?

   ···Oishii ne.

6. Ashita hima?

   ···Un, hima da yo.

7. Kinō no shiken wa dō datta?

   ···Muzukashikatta.

8. Kanji o kaku koto ga dekiru?

   ···Uun, dekinai.

9. Chotto hasami o kashite.

   ···Un.   Demo, boku mo iru kara, ato de kaeshite.

Kaiwa

Pātii

Tanaka : Moshi moshi, Hayashi-san desu ka.

Hayashi no
otōto : Hai, sō desu.

Tanaka : Tanaka desu ga, Ichirō-san o onegai-shimasu.

Tanaka : A, Hayashi-kun.　Ashita no ban hima?

Hayashi : Un, hima da yo.　Dōshite?

Tanaka : Pātii ni ikanai?

Hayashi : Ii ne.　Basho wa doko?

Tanaka : Fuji-hoteru.　6-ji goro hoteru no robii de matte iru yo.

Hayashi : Wakatta.　Ja, mata ashita.

Renshū A

1.

Futsū-kei

kakimasu	kaku	kaka nai	kai ta	kaka nakatta
*arimasu	aru	nai	at ta	nakatta
tabemasu	taberu	tabe nai	tabe ta	tabe nakatta
shimasu	suru	shi nai	shi ta	shi nakatta
kimasu	kuru	ko nai	ki ta	ko nakatta

atsui desu	atsu i	atsu kunai	atsu katta	atsu kunakatta
yasui desu	yasu i	yasu kunai	yasu katta	yasu kunakatta
ii desu	i i	yo kunai	yo katta	yo kunakatta

hima desu	hima da	hima dewa nai (ja)	hima datta	hima dewa nakatta (ja)
ame desu	ame da	ame dewa nai (ja)	ame datta	ame dewa nakatta (ja)

2. Boku wa

kuruma ga	aru.
kinō Tōkyō e	itta.
kamera ga	hoshii.
supōtsu ga	suki da.

3. Boku wa

Sentā ni	sunde iru.
hayaku uchi e	kaeranakereba naranai.
hiragana o	kaku koto ga dekiru.
Nihon no eiga o	mita koto ga nai.

Renshū B

1. Rei : Konban tegami o kaku. ······Konban tegami o kakimasu.
   1）Kōhii o nomu. ······
   2）Asagohan o tabenakatta. ······
   3）Senshū Nihon e kita. ······
   4）Ima okane ga nai. ······

2. Rei : Terebi o mimasu. ······Terebi o miru.
   1）Kōgi o kikimashita. ······
   2）Pasupōto ga irimasu. ······
   3）Rao-san wa heya ni imasen. ······
   4）Kinō doko mo ikimasendeshita. ······

3. Rei : Kono hon wa omoshirokunai desu. ······Kono hon wa omoshirokunai.
   1）Rajikase ga hoshii desu. ······
   2）Kono kamera wa yokunai desu. ······
   3）Ryokō wa tanoshikatta desu. ······
   4）Kinō wa atsukunakatta desu. ······

4. Rei : Kyōto wa shizuka desu. ······Kyōto wa shizuka da.
   1）Kinō wa ame deshita. ······
   2）Sakana ga suki desu. ······
   3）Kyō wa hima dewa arimasen. ······
   4）Kinō wa yasumi dewa arimasendeshita. ······

5. Rei : Terebi o mite imasu. ······Terebi o mite iru.

   1) Kyōto e ikitai desu. ······

   2) Kono heya ni haitte mo ii desu. ······

   3) Mainichi benkyō-shinakereba narimasen. ······

   4) Shinkansen ni notta koto ga arimasen. ······

6. Rei : Nihon-go ga wakarimasu ka. ······Nihon-go ga wakaru?

   1) Kono tokei wa ikura desu ka. ······

   2) Rao-san wa doko ni imasu ka. ······

   3) Ashita hima desu ka. ······

   4) Ryokō wa dō deshita ka. ······

7. Rei : Doko de gohan o taberu? (Sentā no shokudō)
        ······Sentā no shokudō de taberu.

   1) Maiasa nan-ji goro okiru? (6-ji goro) ······

   2) Itsu Nihon e kita? (sengetsu) ······

   3) Kōhii to kōcha to, dotchi ga ii? (kōcha) ······

   4) Kinō doko e itta? (doko mo) ······

8. Rei : Kōbe e itta koto ga aru? (uun) ······Uun, nai.

   1) Tabako o sutte mo ii? (un) ······

   2) Tanaka-san o shitte iru? (uun) ······

   3) Kaisha ni repōto o dasanakereba naranai? (un) ······

   4) Hiragana o kaku koto ga dekiru? (uun) ······

20

166

Renshū C

1. A : Kinō hajimete <u>Nihon no eiga o mita</u> yo.
   　　　　　　　　　　①
   B : Dō datta?

   A : <u>Totemo omoshirokatta.</u>
   　　②

   1) ① hiragana o benkyō-shimashita
   　　 ② yasashikatta desu
   2) ① Kyōto e ikimashita
   　　 ② totemo kirei deshita
   3) ① sashimi o tabemashita
   　　 ② amari oishikunakatta desu

2. A : Ima nani o shite iru?
   B : <u>Tegami o kaite iru.</u>
   A : Ja, ato de kaimono ni ikanai?
   B : Un, ii ne.

167

   1) hon o yonde imasu
   2) heya o sōji-shite imasu
   3) tēpu o kiite imasu

3. A : <u>Nihon-go no jisho</u> o motte iru?
   B : Un, motte iru yo.
   A : Ja, chotto kashite.
   B : Ii yo.

   1) tēpu-rekōdā
   2) hasami
   3) Tōkyō no chizu

Mondai

1. 1) _____
    2) _____
    3) _____
    4) _____
    5) _____

2.

1) Kinō $\begin{cases} \text{a. dekakemashita.} \\ \text{b. Tōkyō e ikimashita.} \\ \text{c. doko mo ikimasendeshita.} \end{cases}$ Heya de (   ).

2) $\begin{cases} \text{a. Korekara tēpu o kikimasu} \\ \text{b. Ima tēpu o kiite imasu} \\ \text{c. Mō tēpu o kikimashita} \end{cases}$ kara, ato de (   ) ni ikimasu.

3) Fuji-hoteru wa $\begin{cases} \text{a. kirei desu.} \\ \text{b. shizuka desu.} \\ \text{c. yūmei desu.} \end{cases}$ Soshite ryōri ga totemo (   ).

4) Shiken wa (   ) kara, $\begin{cases} \text{a. yoku wakarimashita.} \\ \text{b. daitai wakarimashita.} \\ \text{c. zenzen wakarimasendeshita.} \end{cases}$

5) Watashi mo Nihon-go no jisho ga (   ) kara,

$\begin{cases} \text{a. ato de} \\ \text{b. ashita} \\ \text{c. asatte} \end{cases}$ kaeshite kudasai.

3.

Rei : ikimasu		iku	ikanai	itta	ikanakatta
I	hanashimasu				
	machimasu				
	yomimasu				
	*arimasu				
	kaerimasu				
	kaimasu				
	yobimasu				
II	tabemasu				
	imasu				
III	shimasu				
	kimasu				
	samui desu				
	ii desu				
	kirei desu				
	tenki desu				

4. Rei : Resutoran e gohan o <u>tabe ni ikimasu</u>. (tabe ni iku)

1) Nihon e denki no <u>jisshū ni kimashita</u>. (   )

2) Ima hon o <u>yonde imasu</u>. (   )

3) Watashi wa kamera o <u>motte imasen</u>. (   )

4) Mainichi <u>benkyō-shinakereba narimasen</u>. (   )

5) Do-yōbi no gogo <u>benkyō-shinakute mo ii desu</u>. (   )

6) Amari Nihon-go o <u>hanasu koto ga dekimasen</u>. (   )

7) Ichido mo Nihon-ryōri o <u>tabeta koto ga arimasen</u>. (   )

8) Yasukute ii kamera ga <u>hoshii desu</u>. (   )

9) Kōhii o <u>nomitai desu</u>. (   )

10) Enpitsu de <u>kaite mo ii desu</u>. (   )

5.

Kesa hayaku <u>okita</u> (Rei : okimashita).   Ii <u>tenki datta</u> (   ).

Okite kara, kōen e sanpo ni <u>itta</u> (   ).   Kōen wa asa itsumo

<u>shizuka da</u> (   ).   Kōen ni dare mo <u>inakatta</u>(   ).

Sanpo-shite kara,   Sentā e kaette, asagohan o <u>tabeta</u> (   ).

Totemo <u>oishikatta</u> (   ). 9-ji kara shiken ga <u>atta</u> (   ).

Totemo <u>muzukashikatta</u> (   ) kara, amari <u>wakaranakatta</u>(   ).

Dai 21 ka

Bunkei

1. Konban ame ga furu to omoimasu.
2. Kaisha no hito wa ashita Sentā e kuru to iimashita.

Reibun

1. Kagi wa doko desu ka.

   ···Sono kaban no naka ni aru to omoimasu.

2. Kaisha no hito wa pātii ni kimasu ka.

   ···Iie, tabun konai to omoimasu.

3. Tanaka-san wa jimusho ni imasu ka.

   ···Mō uchi e kaetta to omoimasu.   Kaban ga arimasen kara.

4. Kengaku wa dō desu ka.

   ···Omoshiroi desu.

   Keredomo, shitsumon no jikan ga mijikai to omoimasu.

5. Nihon ni tsuite dō omoimasu ka.

   ···Kōtsū ga benri da to omoimasu.

6. Kinō kaigi de kengaku ni tsuite hanashimashita.

   ···Sō desu ka.   Anata mo iken o iimashita ka.

   Hai.   Kengaku wa minna yokatta to iimashita.

7. Do-yōbi Sentā de pātii ga aru deshō?

   ···Hai, arimasu.

Kaiwa

Kaigi

Tanaka : Kengaku ni tsuite nanika iken ga arimasu ka.

Narong : Kengaku wa minna yokatta desu.

Rao　　 : Watashi mo sō omoimasu.

　　　　　Nihon wa hontō ni gijutsu ga susunde iru to omoimasu.

Tanaka : Korekara donna kōjō o kengaku-shitai desu ka.

Narong : Watashi wa mō sukoshi chiisai kōjō o kengaku-shitai desu.

Tanaka : Sō desu ka.　Hoka no minasan wa dō desu ka.

Minna　 : Watashi-tachi mo onaji iken desu.

Renshū A

1.

Ashita ame ga	furu	to omoimasu.
Rao-san wa Sentā ni	inai	
Tanaka-san wa mō uchi e	kaetta	
Nihon wa mono ga	takai	
Nihon wa kōtsū ga	benri da	

2.

Rao-san wa	konban	dekakeru	to iimashita.
	ashita doko mo	ikanai	
	mō ano eiga o	mita	
	mainichi	isogashii	
	do-yōbi wa	hima da	

3.

Ashita pātii ga	aru	deshō?
Pasupōto o	motte iru	
Tōkyō wa hito ga	ōi	
Han-san wa Nihon-go ga	jōzu	

Renshū B

1. Rei : Lee-san wa shinsetsu desu ……Lee-san wa shinsetsu da to omoimasu.
   1) Satō-san wa hontō ni kirei desu ……
   2) Nihon wa denki-seihin ga yasui desu ……
   3) Nihon-jin wa yoku hatarakimasu ……
   4) Ōsaka wa tabemono ga oishii desu ……

2. Rei : Kimura-san wa jimusho ni imasu ka. (hai) ……Hai, iru to omoimasu.
   1) Katō-san wa ashita Sentā e kimasu ka. (iie) ……
   2) Tanaka-san wa mō uchi e kaerimashita ka. (hai, mō) ……
   3) Rao-san wa koibito ga imasu ka. (hai, kitto) ……
   4) Kōjō no hito wa Eigo ga wakarimasu ka. (iie, tabun) ……

3. Rei : Narong-san wa doko ni imasu ka. (robii) ……Robii ni iru to omoimasu.
   1) Koko kara eki made donokurai kakarimasu ka. (20-pun gurai) ……
   2) Narong-san to Rao-san to, dochira ga wakai desu ka. (Narong-san) ……
   3) Hasami wa doko ni arimasu ka. (hako no naka) ……
   4) Nihon ni tsuite dō omoimasu ka. (kōtsū ga benri) ……

4. Rei : ashita shiken ga arimasu
       ……Narong-san wa ashita shiken ga aru to iimashita.
   1) hayaku kuni e kaeritai desu ……
   2) o-sake ga amari suki dewa arimasen ……
   3) kengaku wa minna yokatta desu ……
   4) kōgi wa yaku ni tachimasu ……

5. Rei : Lee-san wa nan-ji goro kaerimasu ka. (8-ji goro)

······8-ji goro kaeru to iimashita.

1) Ali-san wa doko de matte imasu ka. (eki) ······

2) Rao-san wa itsu Hiroshima e ikimasu ka. (raishū) ······

3) Satō-san wa itsu koko e kimasu ka. (ashita) ······

4) Narong-san wa nan-ji goro dekakemasu ka. (2-ji goro) ······

6. Rei : Indo-ryōri wa karai desu ······Indo-ryōri wa karai deshō?

1) Rao-san wa sukii ni ikimasu ······

2) Katō-san o shitte imasu ······

3) ginkō wa do-yōbi yasumi desu ······

4) pātii wa tanoshikatta desu ······

7. Rei : Tai wa ima atsui deshō? ······Hai, atsui desu.

1) Nihon wa tabemono ga takai deshō? ······

2) Fujisan wa kirei datta deshō? ······

3) Minasan wa raishū kenshū-ryokō ni iku deshō? ······

4) Onaka ga suita deshō? ······

Renshū C

1. A : <u>Sentā no shokuji</u> ni tsuite
   ①
   dō omoimasu ka.

   B : Sō desu ne.

   <u>Oishii desu ga, takai</u> to omoimasu.
   ②

   1)　① kōgi　　② muzukashii desu ga, yaku ni tachimasu

   2)　① kengaku　② omoshiroi desu ga, jikan ga mijikai desu

   3)　① Nihon　② kōtsū ga benri desu ga, takai desu

2. A : Kinō kaigi de <u>kōgi</u> ni tsuite hanashimashita.
   ①
   B : Sō desu ka.　Anata mo iken o iimashita ka.

   A : Hai.　<u>Omoshirokute, yaku ni tatsu</u> to iimashita.
   ②

   1)　① kengaku

   　　② jidōsha no kōjō o mitai desu

   2)　① Nihon-go no benkyō

   　　② shukudai ga ōi desu

   3)　① kenshū-ryokō

   　　② Hiroshima e zehi ikitai desu

3. A : <u>Nihon wa tabemono ga takai</u> deshō?
   ①
   B : Ē, <u>takai</u> desu ne.
   ①
   Demo, <u>totemo oishii</u> to omoimasu.
   ②

   1)　① Nihon-go no benkyō wa muzukashii desu

   　　② totemo omoshiroi desu

   2)　① kinō no kengaku wa omoshirokatta desu

   　　② jikan ga mijikakatta desu

   3)　① Nihon wa kōtsū ga benri desu

   　　② kuruma ga ōi desu kara, abunai desu

Mondai

1. 1) _____
   📼 2) _____
   3) _____
   4) _____
   5) _____

2.
   📼 1) Nihon-go no benkyō wa totemo { a. jōzu desu.
                                        b. omoshiroi desu.
                                        c. muzukashii desu. }

   Kōjō de (   ) to omoimasu.

   2) Rao-san to Narong-san no iken wa { a. onaji desu.
                                         b. chigaimasu.
                                         c. sukoshi chigaimasu. }

   Nihon wa (   ) ga takai desu ga, (   ) ga benri desu.

   3) Kimura-san wa (   ) ni imasen.

      { a. Kyō kaisha o yasumimashita.
        b. Ima jimusho de hataraite imasu.
        c. Mō uchi e kaerimashita. }

   4) Kinō no gogo (   ) ga arimashita.

      { a. Rao-san
        b. Minasan   } wa Tōkyō-denki ga ichiban yokatta to iimashita.
        c. Kōjō no hito }

   5) Kin-yōbi no ban (   ) de pātii ga arimasu ga,

      kaisha no hito wa { a. kitto kuru
                          b. tabun kuru   } to omoimasu.
                          c. tabun konai }

3. Rei : Nihon wa (kirei desu ··· kirei da   ) to omoimasu.
   1) Nihon no tabemono wa dō desu ka.
      ······Oishii desu ga, (takai desu ···   ) to omoimasu.
   2) Ashita ame ga furu to omoimasu ka. ······Iie, (furimasen ···   )
      to omoimasu. Tabun ii (tenki desu ···   ) to omoimasu.

3) Rao-san wa Sentā ni imasu ka. ······Iie, dokoka e (dekakemashita ···

) to omoimasu. Uketsuke ni kagi ga arimasu kara.

4) Anata wa kōgi ni tsuite nanika iken o iimashita ka. ······ Hai, kinō no kōgi

wa totemo (omoshirokatta desu ···   ) to iimashita.

5) Kengaku ni tsuite iken o iimashita ka.

······Hai, mō sukoshi chiisai kōjō o (mitai desu ···   ) to iimashita.

4. Rei : Nichi-yōbi hima deshō? ······Hai, hima desu.

1) Ginkō wa do-yōbi yasumi deshō? ······

2) Kyō no gogo kōgi ga aru deshō? ······

3) Kesa no shiken wa muzukashikatta deshō? ······

4) Kaisha no denwa-bangō o shitte iru deshō? ······

5) Mō bangohan o tabeta deshō? ······

5.

Kyō 2-ji kara kaigi ga arimashita. Nihon-go ya kōgi ni tsuite

hanashimashita. Minna iroirona iken o iimashita. Ali-san wa mō sukoshi

Sentā de Nihon-go o benkyō-shitai to iimashita. Watashi mo sō omoimasu.

Kōgi ni tsuite amari iken ga arimasendeshita. Watashi wa kōgi wa

muzukashii desu ga, yaku ni tatsu to iimashita.

Sorekara kengaku ni tsuite hanashimashita. Minna senshū no jidōsha no

kōjō ga ichiban yokatta to iimashita.

Rei : Kyō 2-ji kara kaigi ga arimashita.   (○)

Kyō 2-ji kara kengaku ga arimashita.   (×)

1) Kaigi de minna amari iken o iimasendeshita.   (   )

2) Watashi wa mō sukoshi Nihon-go o benkyō-shitai to omoimasu.   (   )

3) Watashi wa kōgi wa amari yaku ni tatanai to omoimasu.   (   )

4) Jidōsha no kōjō no kengaku ni tsuite minna no iken wa onaji deshita.

(   )

5) Kaigi de kōgi ya kengaku ya Nihon-go ni tsuite minna to

hanashimashita.   (   )

Dai 22 ka

Bunkei

1. Kore wa watashi ga totta shashin desu.
2. Asoko ni iru hito wa Lee-san desu.

Reibun

1. Kore wa doko de katta kamera desu ka.
   ···Shinjuku de katta kamera desu.

2. Kore wa dare ga kaita e desu ka.   Totemo jōzu desu ne.
   ···Lee-san ga kaita e desu.

3. Ano megane o kakete iru hito wa dare desu ka.
   ···Tanaka-san desu.

4. Senshū kengaku-shita tokoro wa doko desu ka.
   ···Nagoya-jidōsha desu.

5. Kinō mita eiga wa dō deshita ka.
   ···Totemo omoshirokatta desu.

6. Kinō no gogo nani o shimashita ka.
   ···Kuruma no buhin o tsukutte iru kōjō o kengaku-shimashita.

7. Nichi-yōbi issho ni asobi ni ikimasen ka.
   ···Sumimasen.   Nichi-yōbi wa tomodachi ni au yakusoku ga arimasu.

Kaiwa

Shigoto no ato de

Tanaka : Suzuki-san, konban issho ni shokuji ni ikimasen ka.

Suzuki : Ē, ii desu ne.

Tanaka : Kimura-san mo issho ni dō desu ka.

Kimura : Sumimasen.   Konban wa chotto tomodachi ni au
yakusoku ga arimasu kara, mata kondo onegai-shimasu.

Tanaka : Sō desu ka.   Zannen desu ne.

Kimura : Ja, osaki ni shitsurei-shimasu.

Tanaka : Otsukaresama deshita.

22

Renshū A

1. Kore wa

kodomo ga	yomu	hon desu.
sensei ni	karita	
kinō Shinjuku de	katta	

2.

Akai fuku o	kite iru	hito wa dare desu ka.
Sukii ni	ikanai	
Kinō Sentā e	kita	

3. Kinō

Kōbe ni	aru	kōjō o kengaku-shimashita.
jidōsha o	tsukutte iru	
Kim-san ga	jisshū-shite iru	

4.

Tegami o	kaku	jikan ga arimasen.
Hon o	yomu	
Eiga o	mi ni iku	

Renshū B

1. Rei : Tōkyō de kaimashita

   ⋯⋯Kore wa Tōkyō de katta kamera desu.

   1) Tanaka-san ni moraimashita ⋯⋯
   2) Mario-san ni karimashita ⋯⋯
   3) kinō Tōkyō no depāto de kaimashita ⋯⋯
   4) watashi ga Kyōto de torimashita ⋯⋯

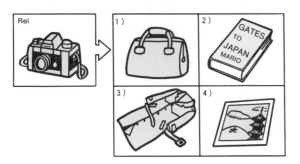

2. Rei : Lee-san wa dono hito desu ka. (biiru)

   ⋯⋯Biiru o nonde iru hito desu.

   1) Rao-san wa dono hito desu ka. (shashin) ⋯⋯
   2) Katō-san wa dono hito desu ka. (isu) ⋯⋯
   3) Tanaka-san wa dono hito desu ka. (megane) ⋯⋯
   4) Ali-san wa dono hito desu ka. (kuroi shatsu) ⋯⋯

3. Rei : (jisshū-shimasu) kōjō wa doko desu ka

    ⋯⋯Jisshū-suru kōjō wa doko desu ka.

    1) (Nihon-go o oshiete imasu) sensei wa donata desu ka ⋯⋯

    2) (kamera o tsukutte imasu) kōjō wa doko desu ka ⋯⋯

    3) (kinō mimashita) eiga wa dō deshita ka ⋯⋯

    4) (Hiroshima de kengaku-shimasu) kōjō wa donna kōjō desu ka ⋯⋯

4. Rei : (kamera o tsukutte imasu) kōjō o kengaku-shimashita

    ⋯⋯Kamera o tsukutte iru kōjō o kengaku-shimashita.

    1) (terebi o mimasu) jikan ga arimasen ⋯⋯

    2) (senshū kaimashita) rajikase o misete kudasai ⋯⋯

    3) (asoko ni arimasu) isu o motte kite kudasai ⋯⋯

    4) (kuruma no buhin o tsukutte imasu) kōjō o kengaku-shitai desu ⋯⋯

5. Rei : Dōshite ikimasen ka. (tomodachi ni aimasu, yakusoku ga arimasu kara)

    ⋯⋯Tomodachi ni au yakusoku ga arimasu kara.

    1) Dōshite kuruma de ikimasen ka.

    (unten-shimasu, hito ga imasen kara) ⋯⋯

    2) Nani o shite imasu ka.

    (kinō kaimashita, tēpu o kiite imasu) ⋯⋯

    3) Dare ni sono tokei o okurimasu ka.

    (sengetsu kekkon-shimashita, tomodachi ni okurimasu) ⋯⋯

    4) Donna kōjō o kengaku-shitai desu ka.

    (robotto o tsukatte imasu, kōjō o kengaku-shitai desu) ⋯⋯

Renshū C

1. A : <u>Suzuki-san</u> wa dono hito desu ka.
      ①
   B : Ano <u>akai sētā o kite iru</u> hito desu.
              ②
   A : Ā, ano hito desu ka.

   1) ① Tanaka-san
        ② megane o kakete imasu
   2) ① Rao-san
        ② kuroi kaban o motte imasu
   3) ① Ali-san
        ② bōshi o kabutte imasu

2. A : <u>Ashita kengaku-suru</u> kōjō wa donna kōjō desu ka.
      ①
   B : <u>Jidōsha o tsukutte iru</u> kōjō de, Nihon de ichiban ōkii
              ②
      mēkā desu.

   1) ① raishū ikimasu
        ② terebi
   2) ① Mario-san ga jisshū-shite imasu
        ② jidōsha no buhin
   3) ① senshū ikimashita
        ② biiru

3. A : Konban nomi ni ikimasen ka.
   B : Sumimasen. Konban wa tomodachi to <u>dekakeru</u> yakusoku ga arimasu.
   A : Sō desu ka. Zannen desu ne.

   1) eiga o mimasu
   2) kaimono ni ikimasu
   3) shokuji-shimasu

Mondai

1. 1) _____
   2) _____
   3) _____
   4) _____
   5) _____

2.
   1) Kore wa (   ) ga
      - a. Kyōto e itta
      - b. Kyōto de totta   shashin desu.
      - c. Kyōto de katta

   2) Hayashi-san wa kuroi (   ) o kite,
      - a. megane o kakete iru
      - b. bōshi o kabutte iru   hito desu.
      - c. kaban o motte iru

   3) Kinō kengaku-shita tokoro wa ATP de, jidōsha no (   ) o
      - a. tsukutte iru
      - b. tsukatte iru   kaisha desu.
      - c. utte iru

   4) Kinō Shinjuku de mita (   ) wa
      - a. totemo kirei deshita.
      - b. totemo omoshirokatta desu.
      - c. amari omoshirokunakatta desu.

   5) Konban wa
      - a. shokuji ni iku
      - b. kaisha no hito ni au   (   ) ga arimasu kara,
      - c. eiga o miru

      issho ni shokuji ni iku koto ga dekimasen.

3. Rei : Asoko ni suwatte iru hito wa [dare   ] desu ka. ······Suzuki-san desu.
   1) Sore wa [   ] de katta kamera desu ka.
      ······Shinjuku de katta kamera desu.
   2) Kore wa [   ] ga totta shashin desu ka.
      ······Watashi ga totta shashin desu.
   3) Kore wa [   ] totta shashin desu ka.
      ······3-nen mae ni totta shashin desu.

4) Ano akai fuku o kite iru hito wa [   ] desu ka. ······Satō-san desu.

5) Senshū kengaku-shita kōjō wa [   ] desu ka.

     ······Nagoya-jidōsha desu.

6) Kinō kiita kōgi wa [   ] deshita ka.

     ······Totemo omoshirokatta desu.

7) Ima ichiban hoshii mono wa [   ] desu ka. ······Bideo desu.

8) Mirion wa [   ] o tsukutte iru kaisha desu ka.

     ······Kamera o tsukutte iru kaisha desu.

9) [   ] kōjō o kengaku-shitai desu ka.

     ······Robotto o tsukatte iru kōjō o kengaku-shitai desu.

10) Kono kōjō de hataraite iru hito wa [   ] desu ka.

     ······1,500-nin gurai desu.

4.

> Raishū no getsu-yōbi kara moku-yōbi made kenshū-ryoko ni ikimasu.
> Getsu-yōbi Nagoya de jidōsha o tsukutte iru kōjō o kengaku-shimasu.
> Sorekara shinkansen de Kyōto e itte, Kyōto-eki no chikaku ni aru hoteru ni
> tomarimasu.　Ka-yōbi Kyōto o kenbutsu-shimasu.　Kyōto wa kireina machi
> desu kara, mitai tokoro ga takusan arimasu.　Demo, amari miru jikan ga
> arimasen kara, zannen desu.
>
> 　Sui-yōbi Ōsaka de konpyūtā no kaisha o kengaku-shimasu.　Kono kaisha
> wa ima Yang-san ga jisshū-shite iru kaisha desu. Yang-san wa Chūgoku no
> daigaku de issho ni benkyō-shita tomodachi desu.　Sorekara gogo Hiroshima
> e ikimasu.　Moku-yōbi Hiroshima kara shinkansen de kaerimasu.

1) Nagoya de kengaku-suru kōjō wa donna kōjō desu ka.

_____

2) Kyōto de tomaru hoteru wa doko ni arimasu ka.

_____

3) Kyōto o kenbutsu-suru jikan ga takusan arimasu ka.

_____

4) Yang-san ga jisshū-shite iru kaisha wa nan no kaisha desu ka.

_____

5) Yang-san wa ima issho ni benkyō-shite iru tomodachi desu ka.

_____

Fukushū D

1.

Rei :
$\begin{Bmatrix} \text{a. Chotto} \\ \text{b. Hayaku} \\ \text{c. Motto} \end{Bmatrix}$ matte kudasai.

1) Mō hirugohan o tabemashita ka. ······Iie, $\begin{Bmatrix} \text{a. mō} \\ \text{b. mada} \\ \text{c. itsumo} \end{Bmatrix}$ desu.

2) Kyō wa $\begin{Bmatrix} \text{a. taihen} \\ \text{b. tokidoki} \\ \text{c. amari} \end{Bmatrix}$ samukunai desu.

3) Nihon-go ga $\begin{Bmatrix} \text{a. yoku} \\ \text{b. takusan} \\ \text{c. zenzen} \end{Bmatrix}$ wakarimasu.

4) Chūgoku wa Nihon yori $\begin{Bmatrix} \text{a. takusan} \\ \text{b. ichiban} \\ \text{c. zutto} \end{Bmatrix}$ ōkii desu.

5) Wakarimasen kara, $\begin{Bmatrix} \text{a. massugu} \\ \text{b. yukkuri} \\ \text{c. hayaku} \end{Bmatrix}$ hanashite kudasai.

6) Kabuki o ichido mo mita koto ga arimasen kara, $\begin{Bmatrix} \text{a. zehi} \\ \text{b. hajimete} \\ \text{c. zenbu de} \end{Bmatrix}$

mitai desu

7) Rao-san wa $\begin{Bmatrix} \text{a. daitai} \\ \text{b. zehi} \\ \text{c. tabun} \end{Bmatrix}$ heya de nete iru to omoimasu.

8) Fujisan wa $\begin{Bmatrix} \text{a. hontō ni} \\ \text{b. mō} \\ \text{c. dandan} \end{Bmatrix}$ kirei da to omoimasu.

2.

1) Ryokō wa tanoshikatta desu. $\begin{Bmatrix} \text{a. Soshite} \\ \text{b. Demo,} \\ \text{c. Sorekara} \end{Bmatrix}$ tsukaremashita.

2) Kōjō no hito wa Eigo ga wakarimasen. $\left\{\begin{array}{l}\text{a. Soshite}\\\text{b. Desukara,}\\\text{c. Demo,}\end{array}\right\}$ Nihon-go de

hanasanakereba narimasen.

3) Kinō depāto de kaimono-shimashita. $\left\{\begin{array}{l}\text{a. Desukara,}\\\text{b. Ja,}\\\text{c. Sorekara}\end{array}\right\}$ eiga o

mimashita.

4) A : Nichi-yōbi hima desu ka.

    B : Hai, hima desu.

    A : $\left\{\begin{array}{l}\text{a. Ja,}\\\text{b. Desukara,}\\\text{c. Sorekara}\end{array}\right\}$ issho ni Kyōto e ikimasen ka.

D

3.

Rei : hatarakimasu	hataraku	hatarakanai	hataraita	hatarakanakatta
kakimasu				
ikimasu				
isogimasu				
nomimasu				
asobimasu				
torimasu				
kaimasu				
tachimasu				
hanashimasu				
tabemasu				
oboemasu				
mimasu				
dekimasu				
benkyō-shimasu				
(Nihon e) kimasu				
arimasu				
ii desu				
ikitai desu				
hima desu				
ame desu				

Dai 23 ka

Bunkei

1. Gaikoku e iku toki, pasupōto ga irimasu.
2. Kono botan o osu to, kikai ga ugokimasu.

Reibun

1. Kaisha e iku toki, itsumo nan de ikimasu ka.
   ···Basu de ikimasu.

2. Okane ga nai toki, dō shimasu ka.
   ···Tomodachi ni karimasu.

3. Itsu kono shashin o torimashita ka.
   ···Senshū Tōkyō e itta toki, torimashita.

4. Shigoto wa nan-ji made desu ka.
   ···5-ji made desu.   Demo, isogashii toki, 10-ji goro made
   hatarakimasu.

5. Himana toki, itsumo nani o shimasu ka.
   ···Terebi o mitari, hon o yondari shimasu.

6. Yoku sukii ni ikimasu ka.
   ···Iie.   Gakusei no toki, yoku ikimashita ga, ima wa amari
   ikimasen.

7. Dōyatte oto o chōsetsu-shimasu ka.
   ···Kore o mawasu to, chōsetsu ga dekimasu.

8. Nihon-go ga wakaranai to, kōjō e itte, komarimasu yo.
   ···Hai, ganbarimasu.

9. Eki wa doko desu ka.
   ···Kono michi o massugu iku to, migi ni arimasu.

Kaiwa

Jidō-kenbaiki

Rao : Shinjuku made ikura desu ka.

Satō : 230-en desu.

Rao : Komatta na.　Komakai okane ga arimasen.

Satō : Daijōbu desu yo.

Koko ni sen-en satsu o irete, 230-en no botan o osu to,

kippu to otsuri ga demasu.

Rao : Kono botan wa nan ni tsukaimasu ka.

Satō : Onaji kippu o 2-mai kau toki, tsukaimasu.

Renshū A

1.

	Jisshū-suru	toki,	Nihon-go de hanasanakereba narimasen.
Imi ga	wakaranai		jisho o mite kudasai.
Kyōto e	itta		kono omiyage o kaimashita.

2.

Sabishi	i	toki,	tomodachi to o-sake o nomimasu.
Hima	na		hon o yomimasu.
Kodomo	no		Manila ni sunde imashita.

3.

Kono botan o	osu	to,	kikai ga tomarimasu.
Nihon-go ga	wakaranai		kōjō de komarimasu.
Hidari e	magaru		eki ga arimasu.

23

Renshū B

1. Rei : heya o demasu, denki o keshite kudasai

  ……Heya o deru toki, denki o keshite kudasai.

  1) kenshū-ryokō ni ikimasu, kamera o motte ikimasu ……

  2) tsukai-kata ga wakarimasen, watashi ni kiite kudasai ……

  3) Ginza e ikimashita, kono nekutai o kaimashita ……

  4) densha o orimasu, kasa o wasurenai de kudasai ……

  5) kikai o tomemasu, kono botan o oshite kudasai ……

2. Rei : samui desu, atatakai ryōri o tabemasu

  ……Samui toki, atatakai ryōri o tabemasu.

  1) nemui desu, kōhii o nomimasu ……

  2) nimotsu ga ōi desu, takushii de ikimasu ……

  3) hima desu, eiga o mi ni ikimasu ……

  4) koshō desu, sugu watashi o yonde kudasai ……

  5) yasumi desu, Tōkyō e asobi ni ikimasu ……

3. Rei : Michi ga wakaranai toki, dō shimasu ka. ······Chizu o mimasu.

1) Sabishii toki, dō shimasu ka. ······

2) Byōki no toki, dō shimasu ka. ······

3) Imi ga wakaranai toki, dō shimasu ka. ······

4) Otsuri ga denai toki, dō shimasu ka. ······

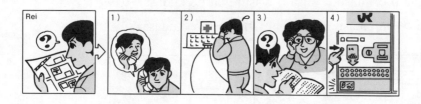

4. Rei : kore o hidari e mawashimasu, oto ga chiisaku narimasu

······ Kore o hidari e mawasu to, oto ga chiisaku narimasu.

1) akai botan o oshimasu, kikai ga tomarimasu ······

2) kore o migi e mawashimasu, oto ga ōkiku narimasu ······

3) pasupōto o nakushimasu, komarimasu ······

4) Nihon-go ga dekimasen, komarimasu ······

5. Rei : massugu ikimasu, eki ga arimasu

······Massugu iku to, eki ga arimasu.

1) ano hashi o watarimasu, byōin ga arimasu ······

2) asoko o migi e magarimasu, kōjō ga arimasu ······

3) shingō o hidari e magarimasu, sūpā ga arimasu ······

4) kono michi o massugu ikimasu, hidari ni ginkō ga arimasu ······

Renshū C

1. A : Sumimasen. <u>Tēpu-rekōdā</u> o kashite kudasai.
   　　　　　　　 ①
   B : Dōzo.

   A : <u>Tēpu o ireru</u> toki, dō shimasu ka.
   　　 ②
   B : Koko o oshite kudasai.

   1)　① kamera　② firumu o iremasu
   2)　① rajio　② oto o chōsetsu-shimasu
   3)　① rajikase　② rajio o kikimasu

2. A : Sumimasen. <u>Kikai ga ugoki</u>masen.
   B : Kono botan o osu to, <u>ugoki</u>masu yo.
   A : Hai, wakarimashita.

   1)　kikai ga tomarimasu
   2)　oto ga ōkiku narimasu
   3)　otsuri ga demasu

3. A : Chotto sumimasen. <u>Ginkō</u> wa doko desu ka.
   　　　　　　　　　　　 ①
   B : <u>Ginkō</u> desu ka.　Asoko ni shingō ga arimasu ne.
   　　 ①
   A : Ē.

   B : Asoko o <u>wataru</u> to, migi ni arimasu.
   　　　　　　 ②

   1)　① yūbinkyoku　② hidari e magarimasu
   2)　① sūpā　② migi e magarimasu
   3)　① Tōkyō-byōin　② watatte, massugu ikimasu

Mondai

1. 1) _____

   🔊 2) _____

   3) _____

   4) _____

   5) _____

2. 🔊 1) Shigoto ga { a. sukunai
                       b. isogashii
                       c. himana } toki, (   ) goro made hatarakimasu.

   2) Satō-san wa itsumo (   ) uchi e kaerimasu ga,

      { a. nimotsu ga ōi
         b. jikan ga nai
         c. ame no } toki, takushii de kaerimasu.

   3) Tanaka-san wa kodomo no toki, (   ) ni { a. sunde imasu.
                                                        b. sunde imashita.
                                                        c. sumitai desu. }

   4) Kono (   ) o osu to, kikai ga { a. tomemasu.
                                               b. tomarimasu.
                                               c. ugokimasu. }

   5) Eki wa (   ) o watatte, { a. massugu iku
                                         b. migi e magaru
                                         c. hidari e magaru } to, migi ni arimasu.

3. Rei : Samui toki, takusan fuku o kimasu.

   1) Tomodachi ga kekkon-suru toki, _____.

   2) Gaikoku e iku toki, _____.

   3) Kotoba no imi ga wakaranai toki, _____.

   4) Sabishii toki, _____.

   5) Byōki no toki, _____.

23

194

4. Rei : Denki o kesu to, (b   )

    1) Nihon-go ga wakaranai to, (   )

    2) Oto ga chiisai toki, kore o migi e
         mawasu to, (   )

    3) Kono michi o massugu iku to, (   )

    4) Kikai o tomeru toki, kono akai
         botan o osu to, (   )

    5) Koko ni okane o irete, botan o
         osu to, (   )

    a. oto ga ōkiku narimasu.

    b. heya ga kuraku narimasu.

    c. migi ni eki ga arimasu

    d. kippu to otsuri ga demasu

    e. kōjō e itte, komarimasu.

    f. kikai ga tomarimasu.

5. | Watashi no uchi wa eki kara aruite 15-fun
    gurai desu.   Eki no mae ni depāto to
    ginkō ga arimasu.   Sono aida no michi o
    massugu iku to, shingō ga arimasu.   Sono
    shingō o hidari e magatte kudasai.

    Sukoshi iku to hashi ga arimasu.   Hashi
    o wataru to, sugu migi ni kōjō ga arimasu.
    Soko o migi e magatte, 2-fun gurai aruku to,
    chiisai kōen ga arimasu.

    Watashi no uchi wa sono tonari desu.

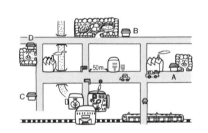

    1) Watashi no uchi wa A, B, C, D no dore desu ka. ······ (   )

    2) Eki kara massugu iku to, shingō ga arimasu.
         Soko o watatte, massugu iku to, nani ga arimasu ka.

    _____

    3) Eki kara yūbinkyoku made, dōyatte ikimasu ka.

    _____

    _____

    _____

Dai 24 ka

Bunkei

1. Kimura-san wa watashi ni nekutai o kuremashita.
2. Watashi wa Kimura-san ni kasa o kashite agemashita.
3. Watashi wa Suzuki-san ni Nihon-go o oshiete moraimashita.
4. Kanai wa watashi ni kodomo no shashin o okutte kuremashita.

Reibun

1. Ii nekutai desu ne.

   ···Kore desu ka.   Kanai ni moraimashita.

   Kanai wa tanjōbi ni itsumo purezento o kuremasu.

2. Kireina shatsu desu ne.   Doko no desu ka.

   ···Indoneshia no shatsu desu.

   Konoaida Ali-san ga kuremashita.

3. Ame ga futte imasu ne.   Kasa o motte kimasendeshita.

   ···Ja, watashi no o kashite agemashō ka.

   Ē, onegai-shimasu.

4. Ashita Yokohama-kōen e ikimasu.

   ···Sō desu ka.   Michi ga wakarimasu ka.

   Ē.   Kimura-san ni oshiete moraimashita.

5. Ashita Nagoya no kōjō e jisshū ni ikimasu.

   ···Sō desu ka.   Dare ga tsurete itte kuremasu ka.

   Takahashi-san ga tsurete itte kuremasu.

Kaiwa

Nihon-go no benkyō

Hayashi : Ima made donokurai Nihon-go o benkyō-shimashita ka.

Rao : Indo de 2-shūkan gurai kaisha no hito ni oshiete moraimashita.

Sorekara Sentā de 5-shūkan naraimashita.

Hayashi : Hontō desu ka.　Jōzu desu ne.

Hiragana ya katakana mo naraimashita ka.

Rao : Iie.　Korekara jibun de benkyō-shitai to omoimasu.

Hayashi : Sō desu ka.　Ja, ii hon ga arimasu kara, kashite agemasu yo.

Ganbatte kudasai.

Renshū A

1. Tanaka-san wa watashi ni   jisho   o kuremashita.
                                       kaban
                                       meishi

2. Kore wa   Tai no ningyō   desu.   Narong-san   ga kuremashita.
                Indoneshia no shatsu   Ali-san
                Chūgoku no okashi   Lee-san

3. Watashi wa Rao-san ni   tēpu o   kashite   agemashita.
                              hiragana o   oshiete
                              tomodachi o   shōkai-shite

4. Watashi wa Tanaka-san ni   hon o   kopii-shite   moraimashita.
                               shinkansen no jikan o   shirabete
                               Tōkyō-tawā e   tsurete itte

5. Katō-san wa watashi ni   chizu o   kaite   kuremashita.
                             okashi o   motte kite
                             kōjō ni tsuite   setsumei-shite

Renshū B

1. Rei :　watashi wa kanai ni nekutai o moraimashita
　　　　　……Kanai wa watashi ni nekutai o kuremashita.
　　1)　watashi wa Ali-san ni tabako o moraimashita ……
　　2)　watashi wa Lee-san ni sētā o moraimashita ……
　　3)　watashi wa Tanaka-san ni jisho o moraimashita ……
　　4)　watashi wa Kimura-san ni ningyō o moraimashita ……

2. Rei :　Ii nekutai desu ne. (koibito) ……Ē, koibito ga kuremashita.
　　1)　Ii bōrupen desu ne. (tomodachi) ……
　　2)　Kireina hana desu ne. (Satō-san) ……
　　3)　Kireina kitte desu ne. (Narong-san) ……
　　4)　Ōkii ringo desu ne. (Kimura-san) ……

3. Rei :　……Watashi wa Rao-san ni kasa o kashite agemashita.
　　1)　……
　　2)　……
　　3)　……
　　4)　……

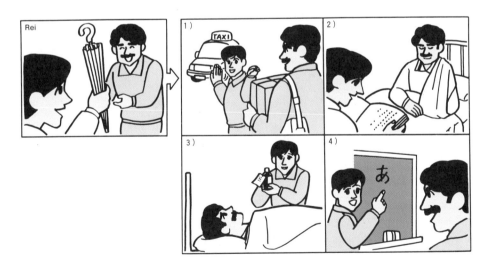

4. Rei :   kasa o kashimasu ……Kasa o kashite agemashō ka.

   1)   nimotsu o mochimasu ……

   2)   shigoto o tetsudaimasu ……

   3)   chizu o kakimasu ……

   4)   takushii o yobimasu ……

5. Rei :   Dare ni Nihon-go o oshiete moraimashita ka. (Suzuki-sensei)
   ……Suzuki-sensei ni oshiete moraimashita.

   1)   Dare ni tēpu-rekōdā o kashite moraimashita ka. (sensei) ……

   2)   Dare ni taipu no tsukai-kata o oshiete moraimashita ka. (Tanaka-san) ……

   3)   Dare ni kōjō o annai-shite moraimashita ka. (Katō-san) ……

   4)   Dare ni kami o kitte moraimashita ka. (Chūgoku no Han-san) ……

6. Rei :   Dare ga okane o haratte kuremashita ka. (Tanaka-san)
   ……Tanaka-san ga haratte kuremashita.

   1)   Dare ga nimotsu o okutte kuremashita ka. (Tanaka-san) ……

   2)   Dare ga Ōsakajō e tsurete itte kuremashita ka. (kaisha no hito) ……

   3)   Dare ga kuruma de okutte kuremashita ka. (Kimura-san) ……

   4)   Dare ga Tōkyō o annai-shite kuremashita ka. (Satō-san) ……

24

Renshū C

1. A : Eki e iku michi ga wakarimasu ka.

   B : Iie, yoku wakarimasen.

   A : Ja, <u>issho ni itte</u> agemashō ka.

   B : Ē, onegai-shimasu.

   1) kuruma de okurimasu

   2) chizu o kakimasu

   3) takushii o yobimasu.

2. A : Kono wāpuro o tsukatte mo ii desu ka.

   B : Sumimasen.　Koshō desu.

   Sugu <u>shūri-shite</u> moraimasu kara, chotto

   matte kudasai.

   1) naoshimasu

   2) shūri ni kimasu

   3) shirabemasu

3. A : <u>Sukiyaki o tabeta</u> koto ga arimasu ka.
   　　　①

   B : Hai, arimasu.

   Konoaida <u>Kimura-san ga tsukutte</u>
   　　　　　　　　　②
   kuremashita.

   1) ① Nihon no eiga o mimasu

   　　② Tanaka-san ga tsurete ikimasu

   2) ① Kyōto e ikimasu

   　　② Suzuki-san ga annai-shimasu

   3) ① Suzuki-san no go-shujin ni aimasu

   　　② Suzuki-san ga shōkai-shimasu

Mondai

1. 1) _____
   🔲 2) _____
   3) _____
   4) _____
   5) _____

2. 1) Katō-san no okusan ga watashi ni kireina (   ) o
   🔲
   $\left\{\begin{array}{l}\text{a. agemashita.}\\\text{b. moraimashita.}\\\text{c. kuremashita.}\end{array}\right\}$

   2) (   ) e iku michi ga wakarimasen kara,

   Rao-san wa $\left\{\begin{array}{l}\text{a. issho ni itte moraimasu.}\\\text{b. hitori de ikimasu.}\\\text{c. chizu de setsumei-shite moraimasu.}\end{array}\right\}$

   3) Kopii no kikai wa ima (   ) desu kara,

   $\left\{\begin{array}{l}\text{a. hoka no kikai de kopii-shite moraimasu.}\\\text{b. tsukai-kata o oshiete moraimasu.}\\\text{c. sugu kikai o naoshite moraimasu.}\end{array}\right\}$

   4) Senshū no nichi-yōbi (   ) ga Lee-san o Ōsakajō e

   $\left\{\begin{array}{l}\text{a. tsurete itte agetai desu.}\\\text{b. tsurete itte moraimashita.}\\\text{c. tsurete itte kuremashita.}\end{array}\right\}$

   5) Shinjuku de (   ) o katte,

   $\left\{\begin{array}{l}\text{a. hitori de motte kimashita.}\\\text{b. tomodachi to issho ni motte kimashita.}\\\text{c. mise no hito ni motte kite moraimashita.}\end{array}\right\}$

24

3. Rei : Tanjōbi ni watashi wa kanai ni nekutai o { (a.) moraimashita. / b. kuremashita. }

1) Ali-san wa watashi ni Indoneshia no tabako o { a. moraimashita. / b. kuremashita. }

2) Kore wa Tanaka-san ni { a. moratta / b. kureta } Nihon-go no jisho desu.

3) Kanai no tanjōbi ni watashi wa fuku o katte { a. agemashita. / b. kuremashita. }

4) Kotoba no imi ga wakaranai toki, sensei ni oshiete { a. moraimasu. / b. kuremasu. }

5) Kodomo no toki, otōsan wa yoku watashi o kōen e tsurete itte { a. moraimashita. / b. kuremashita. }

6) Nihon no tomodachi ga hoshii desu.

    ······Ja, watashi ga ii hito o shōkai-shite { a. agemashō. / b. moraimashō. }

7) Kinō Tanaka-san ni kenshū-ryokō ni tsuite setsumei-shite { a. moraimashita. / b. kuremashita. }

8) Hajimete Sentā e kita toki, Kimura-san ga Sentā o annai-shite { a. moraimashita. / b. kuremashita. }

9) Watashi no kasa o kashite { a. agemashō ka. / b. moraimashō ka. }

    ······Ē, sumimasen ga, kashite kudasai.

10) Otōto wa watashi ni Tai kara shinbun o okutte { a. agemashita. / b. kuremashita. }

4. | Konoaida watashi wa Katō-san no uchi e asobi ni ikimashita. Katō-san no uchi made Tōkyō kara densha de 1-jikan han gurai kakarimashita. Katō-san ni kaite moratta chizu o motte ikimashita. Keredomo, michi ga wakarimasendeshita. Watashi wa michi o aruite iru onna no hito ni michi o kikimashita. Sono onna no hito wa totemo shinsetsuna hito deshita. Watashi o Katō-san no uchi made tsurete itte kuremashita.

Katō-san no okusan wa ryōri ga jōzu de, watashi ni iroirona Nihon-ryōri o tsukutte kuremashita. Hajimete sukiyaki o tabemashita. Totemo oishikatta desu. Shokuji ga owatte kara, watashi no kuni ya Nihon ni tsuite iroiro hanashimashita. Sorekara kōhii o nondari, watashi ga motte itta okashi o tabetari shimashita.

Kaeru toki, sukoshi ame ga futte imashita. Katō-san ga kuruma de eki made okutte kuremashita. Totemo tanoshikatta desu.

Rei : Konoaida Katō-san no uchi e asobi ni ikimashita. (◯)

Kinō Katō-san no uchi e asobi ni ikimashita. (✕)

1) Katō-san no uchi e iku mae ni, chizu o katte, motte ikimashita. ( )

2) Michi ga wakarimasendeshita ga, shinsetsuna otoko no hito ga oshiete kuremashita. ( )

3) Onna no hito ni Katō-san no uchi made tsurete itte moraimashita. ( )

4) Katō-san no okusan ga sukiyaki ya oishii okashi o tsukutte kuremashita.

( )

5) Eki kara Katō-san no uchi made iku toki, aruite ikimashita ga, kaeru toki, kuruma de okutte moraimashita. ( )

Dai 25 ka

Bunkei

1. Ame ga futtara, ikimasen.
2. Ame ga futte mo, ikimasu.

Reibun

1. Nichi-yōbi wa pikunikku desu ne.

   Moshi ame ga futtara, dō shimasu ka.

   ···Ame ga futtara, ikimasen.

2. Basu ga konakattara, dō shimasu ka.

   ···Takushii de ikimashō.

3. Ano mise de ii bideo o utte imasu yo.

   ···Hontō desu ka.   Yasukattara, kaitai desu.

4. Ashita hima dattara, Tōkyō-tawā e ikimasen ka.

   ···Ii desu ne.   Ikimashō.

5. Nan-ji goro kengaku ni ikimasu ka.

   ···Hirugohan o tabetara, sugu ikimasu.

6. Kikai ga ugokimasen.

   ···Suitchi o iremashita ka.

   Hai.   Suitchi o irete mo, ugokimasen.

7. Kono rajikase wa totemo takai desu ne.

   ···Ē.   Demo, ikura takakute mo, kaitai desu.

Kaiwa

Ippan-kenshū ga owatte

Tanaka : Raishū kara jisshū desu ne.

Rao   : Hai.

Tanaka : Kaisha e itte mo, Nihon-go no benkyō o tsuzukete kudasai.

Rao   : Hai, sō shimasu.

Tanaka : Komatta koto ga attara, itsudemo tegami o kaite kudasai.

Rao   : Hai.　Iroiro osewa ni narimashita.

Hontō ni arigatō gozaimashita.

Tanaka : Ja, dōzo o-genki de.　Mata aimashō.

25

207

Renshū A

1.

nomimasu	nonda	ra	nonde	mo
machimasu	matta	ra	matte	mo
tabemasu	tabeta	ra	tabete	mo
mimasu	mita	ra	mite	mo
kimasu	kita	ra	kite	mo
shimasu	shita	ra	shite	mo
atsui desu	atsukatta	ra	atsukute	mo
ii desu	yokatta	ra	yokute	mo
suki desu	suki datta	ra	suki de	mo
kantan desu	kantan datta	ra	kantan de	mo
byōki desu	byōki datta	ra	byōki de	mo
tenki desu	tenki datta	ra	tenki de	mo

2.

Ame ga	futta	ra,	ikimasen.
Jikan ga	nakatta		ikimasen.
	Yasukatta		kaimasu.
	Hima datta		asobi ni kite kudasai.

3.

Ame ga	futte	mo,	ikimasu.
Ikura	takakute		kaimasu.
	Nichi-yōbi de		shigoto o shimasu.

Renshū B

1. Rei : okane ga takusan arimasu, jidōsha o kaitai desu
    ······Okane ga takusan attara, jidōsha o kaitai desu.
    1) jisho o shirabemasu, imi ga wakarimasu ······
    2) Nihon-jin to takusan hanashimasu, Nihon-go ga jōzu ni narimasu ······
    3) machigai ga arimasu, naoshite kudasai ······
    4) kikai ga tomarimasu, sugu suitchi o kitte kudasai ······

2. Rei 1 : yasui desu, kamera o kaimasu ······Yasukattara, kamera o kaimasu.
    Rei 2 : ame desu, dekakemasen ······Ame dattara, dekakemasen.
    1) chikai desu, aruite ikimasu ······
    2) kirai desu, tabenakute mo ii desu ······
    3) atama ga itai desu, heya de yasunde kudasai ······
    4) ashita ii tenki desu, dokoka ikimasen ka ······

3. Rei : Ashita ame ga futtara, dō shimasu ka. ······Doko mo ikimasen.

    1) Okane ga takusan attara, nani o shitai desu ka. ······
    2) Hima dattara, nani o shitai desu ka. ······
    3) Nichi-yōbi tenki ga yokattara, nani o shimasu ka. ······
    4) Kazoku ga Nihon e kitara, doko o annai-shite agetai desu ka. ······

4. Rei : hirugohan o tabemasu, kōjō e kengaku ni ikimasu

   ······Hirugohan o tabetara, kōjō e kengaku ni ikimasu.

   1) kuni e kaerimasu, tegami o kudasai ······

   2) ippan-kenshū ga owarimasu, Hiroshima de jisshū-shimasu ······

   3) kekkon-shimasu, kaisha o yamemasu ······

   4) dōgu o tsukaimasu, sugu katazukete kudasai ······

5. Rei : oboemasu, sugu wasuremasu ······Oboete mo, sugu wasuremasu.

   1) kangaemasu, wakarimasen ······

   2) ame ga furimasu, ikimasu ······

   3) jisho o shirabemasu, wakarimasen ······

   4) kuni e kaerimasu, Nihon-go no benkyō o tsuzukemasu ······

6. Rei 1 : yasui desu, kaimasen ······Yasukute mo, kaimasen.

   Rei 2 : kirai desu, tabemasu ······Kirai de mo, tabemasu.

   1) nemui desu, benkyō-shinakereba narimasen ······

   2) nichi-yōbi desu, hatarakimasu ······

   3) takai desu, sono kamera o kaitai desu ······

   4) shizuka desu, neru koto ga dekimasen ······

7. Rei : Yasukattara, kaimasu ka. ······Iie, yasukute mo, kaimasen.

   1) Jikan ga attara, pātii ni ikimasu ka. ······

   2) Kono hon o mitara, wakarimasu ka. ······

   3) Hima dattara, dekakemasu ka. ······

   4) Kuni e kaettara, Nihon-go no benkyō o yamemasu ka. ······

Renshū C

1. A : Ashita <u>hima dattara</u>, dokoka ikimasen ka.
   　　　　　　①
   B : Ē, doko ga ii desu ka.

   A : <u>Tōkyō-tawā</u> wa dō desu ka.
   　　　②
   B : Ii desu ne.

   1)　① jikan ga arimasu
   　　　② Ōsakajō

   2)　① tenki ga ii desu
   　　　② Fujisan

   3)　① shigoto ga hayaku owarimasu
   　　　② Yokohama-kōen

2. A : Jisshū-suru tokoro wa doko desu ka.
   B : Hiroshima desu.
   A : Itsu ikimasu ka.
   B : <u>Ippan-kenshū ga owattara</u>, sugu ikimasu.

   1)　kenshū-ryokō kara kaerimasu
   2)　hirugohan o tabemasu
   3)　kaisha no hito ga kimasu

3. A : Kikai ga ugokimasen.
   B : <u>Suitchi o iremashita</u> ka.
   A : Ē, <u>irete</u> mo, ugokimasen.
   B : Ja, koshō desu ne.　Sugu shūri-shite moraimashō.

   1)　kono botan o oshimasu
   2)　kore o mawashimasu
   3)　koko o chōsetsu-shimasu

Mondai

1. 1) _____
   2) _____
   3) _____
   4) _____
   5) _____

2.
   1) Nichi-yōbi { a. ii tenki dattara, / b. hima dattara, / c. ame ga futtara, } (   ) ni ikimasu.

   2) { a. Nihon-go no benkyō ga owattara, / b. Kaisha no hito ga kitara, / c. Kenshū-ryōkō kara kaettara, } (   ) e
      jisshū ni ikimasu.

   3) Wāpuro no tsukai-kata ga { a. wakattara, / b. wakaranakattara, / c. warukattara, }
      kono hon de (   ) kudasai.

   4) { a. Ōkute mo, / b. Yasukute mo, / c. Takakute mo, } Nihon no terebi o kaitai desu.
      Watashi no kuni yori zutto (   ) desu kara.

   5) Kono botan o { a. tomete mo, / b. oshite mo, / c. mawashite mo, } (   ) ga demasen.

3.

Rei : ikimasu	ittara	itte mo
kikimasu		
hanashimasu		
machimasu		
nomimasu		
iimasu		
yobimasu		
isogimasu		
mimasu		
(Nihon e) kimasu		
shimasu		

atsui desu	atsukattara	atsukute mo
samui desu		
ii desu		
oishii desu		
isogashii desu		
shizuka desu	shizuka dattara	shizuka de mo
kirei desu		
hima desu		
kantan desu		
tenki desu		

4.   Rei :   Hirugohan o (tabemasu ⋯ tabeta) ra, kōjō e kengaku ni
ikimasu.

1)   Kono repōto ni machigai ga (arimasu ⋯   ) ra, naoshite kudasai.

2)   Ippan-kenshū ga (owarimasu ⋯   ) ra, Ōsaka e jisshū ni ikimasu.

3)   1-ji made ni basu ga (kimasen ⋯   ) ra, takushii de ikimashō.

4)   Ashita (hima desu ⋯   ) ra, watashi no uchi e kimasen ka.

5)   Nichi-yōbi tenki ga (ii desu ⋯   ) ra, Fujisan e ikitai desu.

6)   (Yasui desu ⋯   ) ra, bideo o kaitai desu.

7)   Kono shiken wa muzukashii desu kara, ikura
(kangaemasu ⋯   ) mo, wakarimasen.

8)   Kuni e (kaerimasu ⋯   ) mo, Nihon-go no benkyō o
tsuzukemasu.

9)   Suitchi o (iremasu ⋯   ) mo, kikai ga ugokimasen.

10)   Ashita shiken ga arimasu kara, atama ga
(itai desu ⋯   ) mo, benkyō-shinakereba narimasen.

11)   Do-yōbi (ame desu ⋯   ) mo, sakkā o shimasu.

5.

> Mainichi atsui desu ga, Tanaka-san o-genki desu ka.
>
> Sentā ni iru toki, iroiro osewa ni narimashita.　Hontō ni arigatō gozaimashita.
>
> Ōsaka e kite kara, 1-kagetsu desu.　Gaikoku no kenshūsei wa watashi dake desu kara, sabishii desu.　Demo, kōjō no hito wa minna ii hito desu kara, sabishikute mo, ganbarimasu.
>
> Jisshū wa omoshiroi desu ga, senmon no kotoba wa muzukashii desu. Kōjō no hito wa yoku setsumei-shite kuremasu ga, tokidoki wakarimasen. Wakaranai kotoba ga attara, sugu kaite, yoru heya e kaette kara, jisho de shirabemasu.　Sentā de moratta senmon no kotoba no jisho wa totemo yaku ni tachimasu.
>
> Raigetsu Tōkyō e ikimasu.　Tōkyō e ittara, Tanaka-san ni aitai desu. Moshi hima dattara, issho ni shokuji-shimasen ka.
>
> Dōzo o-genki de.
>
> 　　　　　　　　　　　　　　　　　　　　　　　　　7-gatsu 28-nichi
>
> 　　　　　　　　　　　　　　　　　　　　　　　　　　　　　　Lee

Rei :　Mainichi atsui desu.　　(○)

　　　　Mainichi samui desu.　　(×)

1)　Lee-san wa Sentā o dete, ima Ōsaka de jisshū-shite imasu.　　(　　)

2)　Lee-san wa sabishii desu kara, hayaku kuni e kaeritai desu.　　(　　)

3)　Kōjō no hito ga setsumei-shite mo, hayai desu kara, zenzen wakarimasen.　　(　　)

4)　Kotoba no imi ga wakaranai toki, heya e kaette, jisho de shirabemasu.　　(　　)

5)　Tanaka-san ga Ōsaka e kitara, issho ni shokuji-shimasu.　　(　　)

Fukushū E

1. Rei :   Dōmo arigatō gozaimasu.

   (a. Sayōnara.   b. Genki desu.   ⓒ Dō itashimashite.   )

   1)   Hajimemashite.

   (a. Sō desu ka.   b. Dōzo yoroshiku.   c. Taihen desu ne.   )

   2)   Kagi o onegai-shimasu.

   (a. Hai, sō desu.   b. Hai, dōzo.   c. Iie, kagi dewa arimasen.)

   3)   Kyō wa watashi no tanjōbi desu.

   (a. Omedetō gozaimasu.   b. Shibaraku desu ne.   c. Daijōbu desu.   )

   4)   Kōhii wa ikaga desu ka.

   (a. Hai, kōhii desu.   b. 250-en desu.   c. Itadakimasu.   )

   5)   Dō shimashita ka.

   (a. Ii desu ne.   b. Taihen desu ne.   c. Atama ga itai desu.)

   6)   Itte irasshai.

   (a. Itte mairimasu.   b. Hai, sō desu.   c. Gomen kudasai.   )

   7)   Tadaima.

   (a. Oyasuminasai.   b. Okaerinasai.   c. Sayōnara.   )

   8)   Irasshaimase.

   (a. Kamera o misete kudasai.   b. Mata kimasu.   c. Sō shimashō.   )

   9)   Tanaka-san wa byōki desu kara, pātii ni kimasen.

   (a. Ii desu ne.   b. Hai, dōzo.   c. Zannen desu ne.   )

   10)   Gomen kudasai.

   (a. Daijōbu desu.   b. Irasshai.   c. Sorosoro shitsurei-shimasu.)

   11)   Osaki ni shitsurei-shimasu.

   (a. Otsukaresama deshita.   b. Itadakimasu.   c. Gomen kudasai.   )

   12)   Ashita shiken ga arimasu.

   (a. Shibaraku desu ne.   b. Ganbatte kudasai.   c. Chotto sumimasen.)

   13)   Raishū kuni e kaerimasu.

   (a. Dōzo yoroshiku.   b. Dōzo o-genki de.   c. Okaerinasai.   )

2. Rei : Chotto (machimasu ⋯ matte   ) kudasai.

   1) Ashita ame ga (furimasu ⋯   ) to omoimasu.

   2) Kazoku wa (genki desu ⋯   ) to omoimasu.

   3) Rao-san wa ashita doko mo (ikimasu ⋯   ) to iimashita.

   4) Raishū pātii ga (arimasu ⋯   ) deshō?

   5) Ano megane o (kakete imasu ⋯   ) hito wa dare desu ka.

   6) Senshū (kengaku-shimasu ⋯   ) kōjō wa doko desu ka.

   7) Shinbun o (yomimasu ⋯   ) jikan ga arimasen.

   8) Kyōto e (ikimasu ⋯   ) toki, kono omiyage o kaimashita.

   9) (Hima desu ⋯   ) toki, hon o yomimasu.

   10) (Koshō desu ⋯   ) toki, watashi o yonde kudasai.

   11) Migi e (magarimasu ⋯   ) to, eki ga arimasu.

   12) Nihon-go ga (wakarimasen ⋯   ) to, komarimasu.

   13) Konoaida Kimura-san ni Kōbe e (tsurete ikimasu ⋯   )
       moraimashita.

   14) Tanaka-san wa watashi ni Nihon-go de (setsumei-shimasu ⋯   )
       kuremashita.

   15) Okane ga (arimasu ⋯   ) ra, ryokō-shitai desu.

   16) Takushii ga (kimasen ⋯   ) ra, basu de ikimashō.

   17) (Ame desu ⋯   ) ra, doko mo ikimasen.

   18) Ikura (shirabemasu ⋯   ) mo, wakarimasen.

   19) (Takai desu ⋯   ) mo, kaimasu.

   20) (Nichi-yōbi desu ⋯   ) mo, hatarakimasu.

E

Joshi

1. [wa]

A : 1) Watashi <u>wa</u> Rao desu. (Dai 1 ka)

2) Kono densha <u>wa</u> Tōkyō e ikimasu. (5)

B : 1) Gogo <u>wa</u> kōgi desu. (4)

2) Konban shokuji ni ikimasen ka.

···Konban <u>wa</u> tomodachi ni au yakusoku ga arimasu. (22)

2. [mo]

A : 1) Ano hito wa kenshūsei desu.   Watashi <u>mo</u> kenshūsei desu. (1)

2) Kitte o 2-mai kudasai.   Sorekara fūtō <u>mo</u> kudasai. (11)

3) Ringo to mikan to, dochira ga suki desu ka.

···Dochira <u>mo</u> suki desu. (12)

B : 1) Ashita doko <u>mo</u> ikimasen. (5)

2) Kesa nani <u>mo</u> tabemasendeshita. (6)

3) Niwa ni dare <u>mo</u> imasen. (10)

218

3. [no]

A : 1) Watashi wa Indo <u>no</u> Rao desu. (1)

2) Watashi wa Tōkyō-denki <u>no</u> kenshūsei desu. (1)

3) Kore wa watashi <u>no</u> hon desu. (2)

4) Kore wa Nihon <u>no</u> tokei desu. (3)

5) NTC wa konpyūtā <u>no</u> kaisha desu. (3)

B : 1) Nihon-go <u>no</u> benkyō wa 9-ji kara desu. (4)

2) Taipu <u>no</u> tsukai-kata o oshiete kudasai. (14)

C : 1) Kinō <u>no</u> ban benkyō-shimashita ka. (4)

2) Tsukue <u>no</u> ue ni hon ga arimasu. (10)

D : 1) Kono hon wa watashi <u>no</u> desu. (2)

2) Chiisai <u>no</u> o misete kudasai. (14)

4. [o]

A : 1) Gohan <u>o</u> tabemasu. (6)

2) Tomodachi to pinpon <u>o</u> shimasu. (6)

3) Nihon e kanai <u>o</u> tsurete kimasu. (24)

B : Kaisha <u>o</u> yasumimasu. (9)

C : 1) Heya o demasu. (13)

2) Densha o orimasu. (16)

D : 1) Kōen o sanpo-shimasu. (13)

2) Hashi o watarimasu. (23)

3) Kono michi o massugu iku to, eki ga arimasu. (23)

5. [ga]

A : 1) Watashi wa ringo ga suki desu. (9)

2) Ali-san wa uta ga jōzu desu. (9)

3) Watashi wa kamera ga arimasu. (9)

4) Watashi wa Nihon-go ga wakarimasu. (9)

5) Watashi wa kodomo ga futari imasu. (11)

6) Watashi wa kamera ga hoshii desu. (13)

7) Watashi wa sukii ga dekimasu. (18)

8) Watashi wa tēpu-rekōdā ga irimasu. (20)

B : 1) Watashi wa atama ga itai desu. (9)

2) Han-san wa kami ga nagai desu. (16)

3) Nihon wa kōtsū ga benri desu. (21)

C : 1) Asoko ni otoko no hito ga imasu. (10)

2) Asoko ni ginkō ga arimasu. (10)

3) Ashita Sentā de pātii ga arimasu. (21)

D : 1) Shinkansen to hikōki to, dochira ga hayai desu ka.

···Hikōki no hō ga hayai desu. (12)

2) Kurasu de Narong-san ga ichiban wakai desu. (12)

E : 1) Ima ame ga futte imasu. (14)

2) Shigoto ga owatte kara, sugu uchi e kaerimasu. (16)

3) Kono botan o osu to, kikai ga tomarimasu. (23)

F : 1) Kore wa watashi ga totta shashin desu. (22)

2) Kazoku ga Nihon e kitara, Kyōto e tsurete ikitai desu. (25)

G : Ali-san ga kono shatsu o kuremashita. (24)

6. [ni]

A : 1) Maiasa 6-ji ni okimasu. (4)

2) 9-gatsu 15-nichi ni Nihon e kimashita. (5)

B : 1) Watashi wa tomodachi ni hon o agemashita. (7)

2) Watashi wa kaisha ni denwa o kakemasu. (7)

219

C : 1) Watashi wa Katō-san <u>ni</u> tokei o moraimashita. (7)

2) Watashi wa Suzuki-sensei <u>ni</u> Nihon-go o naraimashita. (7)

D : 1) Tanaka-san wa jimusho <u>ni</u> imasu. (10)

2) Depāto wa eki no mae <u>ni</u> arimasu. (10)

3) Watashi wa Tōkyō <u>ni</u> sunde imasu. (15)

E : 1) Heya <u>ni</u> hairimasu. (13)

2) Kono isu <u>ni</u> suwatte mo ii desu ka. (15)

3) Densha <u>ni</u> horimasu. (16)

4) Kikai <u>ni</u> sawaranai de kudasai. (17)

F : Sukii <u>ni</u> ikimasu. (18)

G : 1) Doru o en <u>ni</u> kaemasu. (18)

2) Lee-san wa byōki <u>ni</u> narimashita. (19)

7. [e]

1) Kyōto <u>e</u> ikimasu. (5)

2) Depāto <u>e</u> kaimono ni ikimasu. (13)

3) Migi <u>e</u> magaru to, ginkō ga arimasu. (23)

8. [de]

A : 1) Densha <u>de</u> Tōkyō e ikimasu. (5)

2) Doraibā <u>de</u> jidōsha o shūri-shimasu. (7)

3) Nihon-go <u>de</u> repōto o kakimasu. (7)

B : Depāto <u>de</u> shatsu o kaimasu. (6)

C : Supōtsu [no naka] <u>de</u> sakkā ga ichiban suki desu. (12)

9. [to]

A : 1) Watashi wa tomodachi <u>to</u> Tōkyō e ikimasu. (5)

2) Rao-san wa kaisha no hito <u>to</u> hanashite imasu. (14)

B : 1) Pan <u>to</u> tamago o tabemasu. (6)

2) Hon-ya wa ginkō <u>to</u> sūpā no aida ni arimasu. (10)

C : Kōhii <u>to</u> kōcha <u>to</u>, dochira ga ii desu ka. (12)

10. [ya]

Heya ni beddo <u>ya</u> tsukue <u>ya</u> isu ga arimasu. (10)

11. [kara] [made]

1) Mainichi 9-ji kara 5-ji made hatarakimasu. (4)

2) Nihon-go no benkyō wa 9-ji kara desu. (4)

3) Depāto wa yoru 7-ji made desu. (4)

4) Tōkyō kara Ōsaka made shinkansen de 3-jikan gurai kakarimasu. (11)

12. [made ni]

12-ji made ni Sentā e kaeranakereba narimasen. (17)

13. [ka]

A : 1) Anata wa Rao-san desu ka. (1)

2) Sore wa bōrupen desu ka, shāpu-penshiru desu ka. (2)

3) Issho ni gohan o tabemasen ka. (6)

B : 1) Kaban-uriba wa doko desu ka.

···Kaban-uriba desu ka.   5-kai desu. (3)

2) Nihon-go no benkyō wa 9-ji kara desu.

···Sō desu ka. (4)

14. [yori]

Indo wa Nihon yori atsui desu. (12)

15. [ne]

1) Benkyō wa 9-ji kara 5-ji made desu.

···Sō desu ka.   Taihen desu ne. (4)

2) Issho ni eiga o mimasen ka.

···Ii desu ne. (6)

3) Nihon-go no benkyō wa dō desu ka.

···Sō desu ne.   Muzukashii desu ga, omoshiroi desu. (8)

16. [yo]

Kono densha wa Yokohama e ikimasu ka.

···Iie, ikimasen.   3-bansen desu yo. (5)

221

Fōmu no tsukai-kata

1. [masu-kei]

masu-kei + mashō	Robii de yasumimashō.	(Dai 6 ka)
masu-kei + masen ka	Issho ni depāto e ikimasen ka.	(6)
masu-kei + tai desu	Gohan o tabetai desu.	(13)
masu-kei + ni ikimasu	Shinjuku e kamera o kai ni ikimasu.	(13)
masu-kei + mashō ka	Takushii o yobimashō ka.	(14)

2. [te-kei]

te-kei + kudasai	Sumimasen ga, jisho o kashite kudasai.	(14)
te-kei + imasu	Ima ame ga futte imasu.	(14)
	Watashi wa kamera o motte imasu.	(15)
te-kei + mo ii desu	Tabako o sutte mo ii desu ka.	(15)
te-kei + kara, ~	Shigoto ga owatte kara, sugu uchi e kaerimasu.	(16)
te-kei, te-kei, ~	Asa okite, gohan o tabete, kaisha e ikimasu.	(16)
te-kei + agemasu	Watashi no kasa o kashite agemasu.	(24)
te-kei + moraimasu	Suzuki-san ni Nihon-go o oshiete moraimashita.	(24)
te-kei + kuremasu	Kanai ga shashin o okutte kuremashita.	(24)

3. [nai-kei]

nai-kei + nai de kudasai	Kōjō no naka de shashin o toranai de kudasai.	(17)
nai-kei + nakereba narimasen	12-ji made ni Sentā e kaeranakereba narimasen.	(17)
nai-kei + nakute mo ii desu	Mainichi repōto o dasanakute mo ii desu.	(17)

4. [jisho-kei]

jisho-kei + koto ga dekimasu	Nihon-go o hanasu koto ga dekimasu.	(18)
jisho-kei + koto desu	Watashi no shumi wa eiga o miru koto desu.	(18)
jisho-kei + mae ni, ~	Bangohan o taberu mae ni, shawā o abimasu.	(18)

5. **[ta-kei]**

ta-kei + koto ga arimasu	Kyōto e itta koto ga arimasu. (19)
ta-kei + ri, **ta-kei** + ri shimasu	Nichi-yōbi sentaku-shitari, sōji-shitari shimasu. (19)

6. **[futsū-kei]**

futsū-kei + to omoimasu	Ashita ame ga furu to omoimasu. (21)
	Nihon wa mono ga takai to omoimasu. (21)
	Nihon wa kōtsū ga benri da to omoimasu. (21)
futsū-kei + to iimasu	Katō-san wa ashita Sentā e kuru to iimashita. (21)

dōshi
i-keiyōshi } **futsū-kei**
na-keiyōshi | **futsū-kei** } +deshō?
meishi } ~d̶a̶

Do-yōbi Sentā de pātii ga aru deshō? (21)

Fujisan wa kirei deshō? (21)

dōshi futsū-kei + **meishi**	Kore wa Tanaka-san ga totta shashin desu. (22)
	Bōshi o kabutte iru hito wa Ali-san desu. (22)

223

7. **dōshi futsū-kei**
  i-keiyōshi ~i } + toki, ~
  na-keiyōshi ~na
  meishi ~no

Gaikoku e iku toki, pasupōto ga irimasu. (23)
Samui toki, sētā o kimasu. (23)
Himana toki, terebi o mimasu. (23)
Gakusei no toki, yoku sukii ni ikimashita. (23)

8. **futsū-kei kako** + ra, ~

Moshi ashita ame ga futtara, pikunikku ni ikimasen. (25)
Yasukattara, kamera o kaitai desu. (25)
Ashita ii tenki dattara, dekakemasu. (25)

9. **dōshi te-kei**
  i-keiyōshi ~kute } + mo, ~
  na-keiyōshi } ~ de
  meishi

Suitchi o irete mo, kikai ga ugokimasen. (25)
Ikura takakute mo, kuruma o kaitai desu. (25)

Ame demo, ryokō ni ikimasu. (25)

10. **jisho-kei** } + to, ~
  nai-kei

Kono botan o osu to, kikai ga tomarimasu. (23)
Nihon-go ga wakaranai to, kōjō de komarimasu. (23)

Fukushi, Fukushi-teki hyōgen

1. **takusan**   Lee-san wa okane ga <u>takusan</u> arimasu.   (Dai 9 ka)

   minna   Kōjō-kengaku wa <u>minna</u> omoshirokatta desu.   (21)

   iroiro   Tomodachi to <u>iroiro</u> hanashimashita.   (16)

   taihen   Indo wa ima <u>taihen</u> atsui desu.   (8)

   totemo   Kyō wa <u>totemo</u> ii tenki desu.   (12)

   yoku   Han-san wa Nihon-go ga <u>yoku</u> wakarimasu.   (9)

   daitai   3-shūkan hiragana o naraimashita.

       Ima hiragana ga <u>daitai</u> wakarimasu.   (9)

   sukoshi   Watashi wa Eigo ga <u>sukoshi</u> wakarimasu.   (9)

   chotto   <u>Chotto</u> matte kudasai.   (2)

   mō sukoshi   Kono kamera wa takai desu.

       <u>Mō sukoshi</u> yasui no wa arimasen ka.   (14)

   zutto   Indo wa Nihon yori <u>zutto</u> ōkii desu.   (12)

   ichiban   Kudamono [no naka] de ringo ga <u>ichiban</u> suki desu.   (12)

2. **itsumo**   Gozen wa <u>itsumo</u> Nihon-go o benkyō-shimasu.   (13)

   tokidoki   Gogo <u>tokidoki</u> kōjō e kengaku ni ikimasu.   (13)

   yoku   Gakusei no toki, <u>yoku</u> sukii ni ikimashita.   (23)

   hajimete   Nihon e kita koto ga arimasen.   <u>Hajimete</u> kimashita.   (19)

   mō ichido   Wakarimasen kara, <u>mō ichido</u> itte kudasai.   (14)

   mata   <u>Mata</u> ashita aimashō.   (14)

3. **ima**   <u>Ima</u> 1-ji han desu.   (4)

       Gakusei no toki, yoku sukii ni ikimashita ga, <u>ima</u> wa amari ikimasen.   (23)

   sugu   Shigoto ga owatte kara, <u>sugu</u> uchi e kaerimasu.   (14)

   mō   <u>Mō</u> hirugohan o tabemashita ka.   (7)

   mada   Iie, <u>mada</u> desu.   (7)

   sorosoro   Mō 9-ji desu kara, <u>sorosoro</u> shitsurei-shimasu.   (19)

korekara	Korekara hirugohan o tabemasu.	(7)
ato de	Ima isogashii desu kara, ato de kite kudasai.	(14)
konoaida	Konoaida Tōkyō-tawā e ikimashita.	(24)

4. issho ni — Issho ni depāto e ikimasen ka. (6)

issho ni	Issho ni depāto e ikimasen ka.	(6)
hitori de	Watashi wa hitori de Nihon e kimashita.	(5)
jibun de	Korekara jibun de hiragana o benkyō-shimasu.	(24)
zenbu de	Watashi no kazoku wa zenbu de 5-nin desu.	(11)

hayaku	Hayaku kyōshitsu e kite kudasai.	(14)
yukkuri	Sumimasen ga, yukkuri hanashite kudasai.	(14)
dandan	Korekara dandan samuku narimasu.	(19)
massugu	Kono michi o massugu iku to, migi ni kōjō ga arimasu.	(23)

5. amari

amari	Kono jisho wa amari yokunai desu.	(8)
zenzen	Watashi wa kanji ga zenzen wakarimasen.	(9)
ichido mo	Nihon-ryōri o ichido mo tabeta koto ga arimasen.	(19)
kitto	Kazoku wa kitto genki da to omoimasu.	(21)
tabun	Ashita tabun ame ga furu to omoimasu.	(21)
moshi	Moshi okane ga takusan attara, kuruma o kaitai desu.	(25)
ikura	Ikura jisho o shirabete mo, imi ga wakarimasen.	(25)
zehi	Shinkansen ni notta koto ga arimasen kara, zehi noritai desu.	(19)

6. mochiron

| mochiron | Lee-san wa Chūgoku-jin desu kara, mochiron kanji ga wakarimasu. | (9) |
| hontō ni | Fujisan wa hontō ni kirei da to omoimasu. | (21) |

225

Setsuzoku no iroiro

1. **soshite**   Kimura-san wa kirei desu.   Soshite taihen shinsetsu desu.   (Dai 8 ka)

   ~ de   Kimura-san wa kirei de, taihen shinsetsu desu.   (16)

   ~ kute   Ano resutoran wa yasukute, oishii desu.   (16)

   sorekara   Kitte o kudasai.   Sorekara kono nimotsu mo onegai-shimasu.   (11)

   ~ tari   Nichi-yōbi kaimono-shitari, eiga o mitari shimasu.   (19)

   ~ ga   Moshi moshi, Tanaka desu ga, Ichirō-san o onegai-shimasu.   (20)

2. **sorekara**   Gohan o tabemasu.   Sorekara terebi o mimasu.   (6)

   ~ te kara   Bangohan o tabete kara, terebi o mimasu.   (16)

   ~ te, ~ te   Bangohan o tabete, terebi o mite, Nihon-go o benkyō-shimasu.   (16)

   ~ mae ni   Neru mae ni, Nihon-go o benkyō-shimasu.   (18)

   ~ toki   Kaisha e iku toki, itsumo densha de ikimasu.   (23)

3. **~ kara**   Shukudai ga takusan arimasu kara, doko mo ikimasen.   (9)

   desukara   Kōjō no hito wa Eigo ga wakarimasen.

   Desukara, Nihon-go de hanasanakereba narimasen.   (17)

4. **~ ga**   Nihon no tabemono wa oishii desu ga, takai desu.   (8)

   demo   Kamera ga hoshii desu.   Demo, okane ga arimasen.   (12)

   keredomo   Kengaku wa omoshiroi desu.

   Keredomo, shitsumon no jikan ga mijikai to omoimasu.   (21)

5. **ja**   A : Kono kaban wa 3,500-en desu.

   B : Ja, sore o kudasai.   (3)

   ~ to   Kono michi o massugu iku to, migi ni kōjō ga arimasu.   (23)

   ~ tara   Moshi ashita ame ga futtara, uchi ni imasu.   (25)

6. **~ te mo**   Ame ga futte mo, ryokō ni ikimasu.   (25)

Sakuin

— A —

A	2
Ā	6
abimasu [shawā o ~]	16
abunai	17
achira	3
agemasu	7
aida	10
aimasu [tomodachi ni ~]	6
akai	8
akarui	16
akemasu	15
amai	12
amari	8
ame	12
Amerika	3
anata	1
annai-shimasu	24
ano ~	2
Anō	10
ano hito	1
aoi	8
araimasu	16
are	2
[Dōmo] arigatō gozaimasu.	2
【Kyō】 wa dōmo arigatō gozaimashita.	19
【Yasui no】 wa arimasen ka.	14

arimasu	9
arimasu	10
aruite	5
arukimasu	16
asa	4
asagohan	6
asatte	4
ashi	16
ashita	4
asobimasu	13
asoko	3
atama	9
atarashii	8
atatakai	12
atchi	20
ato de	14
atsui	8

— B —

ban	4
-ban	16
banana	9
bangohan	6
-bansen	5
basho	20
basu	5
beddo	10

227

benkyō	4	daigaku	15
benkyō-shimasu	4	Daijōbu desu.	18
benri [na]	21	daitai	9
bideo	13	~ dake	11
biiru	6	Dame desu.	17
biru	10	dandan	19
boku	20	dansu	9
bōrupen	2	dare	1
bōshi	22	dashimasu	17
botan	23	dekakemasu	19
buhin	22	dekimasu	18
butaniku	9	demasu [heya o ~]	13
byōin	5	demasu [kippu ga ~]	23
byōki	9	demo	12
		denki	1

228

		densha	5
— C —		denwa	2
		denwa-bangō	14
Chigaimasu.	2	depāto	5
chiisai	8	desukara	17
chikai	12	dō	8
chikaku	10	doa	2
chikatetsu	5	dochira	3
chizu	10	dochira	12
chōsetsu-shimasu	23	dochira mo	12
chotto	2	dōgu	25
Chūgoku	1	Dō itashimashite.	7
		doko	3
— D —		dokoka	13
-dai	11	dokushin	15

Dōmo.	3	Ēto···	16
donata	1		
donna ~	8	— F —	
dono ~	16		
donokurai	11	Firipin	1
doraibā	7	firumu	6
dore	8	fōku	7
doru	18	fuben [na]	21
Dō shimashita ka.	9	Fujisan	8
dōshite	9	fuku	22
dotchi	20	-fun	4
dōyatte	16	fune	5
do-yōbi	4	furimasu [ame ga ~]	14
Dōzo.	2	furui	8
Dōzo kochira e.	8	futari	11
Dōzo o-genki de.	25	futatsu	11
Dōzo yoroshiku.	1	fūtō	11
		futsuka	5

— E —

e	18	— G —	
Ē	6	~ ga	8
ea-mēru	11	gaikoku	19
eiga	6	gakkō	10
Eigo	7	gakusei	15
eki	5	ganbarimasu	23
-en	3	Ganbatte kudasai.	24
enjinia	15	-gatsu	5
enpitsu	2	genki [na]	8
erebētā	3	getsu-yōbi	4

229

gijutsu	21	han	4	
Gijutsu ga susunde imasu.	21	hana	8	
ginkō	5	hana	16	
ginkōin	15	hanashimasu	14	
gitā	9	hanbāgu	16	
go（5）	Ⅳ	hansamu [na]	8	
～ go	7	haraimasu	17	
Gochisōsama [deshita].	8	hasami	7	
gogo	4	hashi	7	
gohan	6	hashi	23	
Gomen kudasai.	19	hatarakimasu	4	
～ goro	16	hatsuka	5	
go-shujin	7	hayai	12	
gozen	4	hayaku	14	
～ gurai	11	herumetto	22	
gyūniku	9	heta [na]	9	
gyūnyū	6	heya	3	
		hidari	10	
		hiitā	17	
― H ―		hikimasu [piano o ～]	18	
		hikōki	5	
		hikui	8	
ha	16	【Ashita】 hima desu ka.	6	
hachi（8）	Ⅳ	hima [na]	12	
hai	1	hiragana	9	
hairimasu [heya ni ～]	13	hiroi	16	
haizara	2	hiru	4	
Hajimemashite.	1	hirugohan	6	
hajimemasu	18	hito	5	
hajimete	19	hitori	11	
hakimasu [kutsu o ～]	22			
hako	2			

hitori de	5	ikura [～ te mo]	25
hitotsu	11	ikutsu	11
hoka no ～	21	ima	4
hon	2	ima	23
Hontō desu ka.	24	imasu	10
hontō ni	21	imasu [kodomo ga ～]	11
hon-ya	5	imasu [Nihon ni ～]	11
hoshii	13	imi	23
hotchikisu	10	imōto	7
hoteru	19	imōto-san	15
hyaku	3	Indo	1
		Indoneshia	1
		ippan-kenshū	25

— I —

		Irasshai [mase].	3
ichi（1）	IV	iremasu	17
ichiban	12	iremasu [suitchi o ～]	25
ichido mo	19	irimasu [jisho ga ～]	20
ichi-nichi (1-nichi)	11	iroiro	16
Igirisu	3	iroiro [na]	10
ii	8	isogashii	12
ii [kōhii ga ～]	12	isogimasu	14
Ii desu ne.	6	issho ni	6
iie	1	isu	2
iimasu	14	Itadakimasu.	8
Ii 【shatsu】 desu ne.	7	itai [atama ga ～]	9
Ii tenki desu ne.	13	itsu	5
【Kōhii】 wa ikaga desu ka.	8	itsudemo	25
iken	21	itsuka	5
ikimasu	5	itsumo	13
ikura	3	itsutsu	11

Itte irasshai.	10	kagi	2
Itte mairimasu.	10	-kai	3
		-kai	11
— J —		kaigi	21
		kaimasu	6
Ja	3	kaimono-shimasu	13
-ji	4	kaisha	3
jibun de	24	kaishain	15
jidōsha	1	kakarimasu	11
jikan	9	kakemasu [denwa o ~]	7
-jikan	11	kakemasu [megane o ~]	22
jimusho	3	kaki-kata	14
~ jin	1	kakimasu	6
jisho	2	kamera	2
jisshū-shimasu	6	kami	2
jōzu [na]	9	kami	16
jū（10）	IV	kanai	7
jūsho	14	kanashii	23
jūsu	6	kangaemasu	25
jū yokka	5	kanji	9
		Kankoku	1
— K —		kantan [na]	18
		kao	16
kaban	2	~ kara	4
kabuki	19	~ kara	9
kaburimasu [bōshi o ~]	22	karada	16
kaemasu	13	karai	12
kaerimasu	5	karimasu	7
kaeshimasu	17	karui	16
-kagetsu	11	kasa	14

232

kasetto-tēpu	6	kirei [na]	8
kashimasu	7	kirimasu	7
katakana	9	kirimasu [suitchi o ～]	25
katazukemasu	25	kitte	11
ka-yōbi	4	kitto	21
Kaze o hikimashita.	9	kōcha	6
kazoku	7	kochira	3
Kekkō desu.	II	Kochira wa ikaga desu ka.	14
kekkon-shimasu	13	kodomo	7
kenbutsu-shimasu [machi o ～]	13	kōen	10
kengaku	4	kōgi	4
kengaku-shimasu [kōjō o ～]	13	kōhii	6
kenshū-ryokō	21	koibito	5
kenshūsei	1	kōjō	5
keredomo	21	koko	3
kesa	4	kokonoka	5
keshigomu	10	kokonotsu	11
keshimasu	15	komakai okane	23
kikai	1	komarimasu	23
kikimasu	6	komatta koto	25
kikimasu [sensei ni ～]	23	Komatta na.	23
kimasu	5	konban	4
kimasu [shatsu o ～]	22	Konbanwa.	III
kimi	20	kongetsu	5
kin'en	15	Konnichiwa.	III
kinō	4	kono ～	2
kin-yōbi	4	konoaida	24
ki o tsukemasu [kuruma ni ～]	17	konpyūtā	1
kippu	11	konshū	5
kirai [na]	9	kopii-shimasu	24

233

kore	2		— M —	
korekara	7			
koshō	18	machi		8
kotae	II	machigai		25
kotchi	20	machimasu		14
kōto	22	mada		7
kotoba	14	Mada mada dame desu.		18
kotoshi	5	～ made		4
kōtsū	21	～ made ni		17
ku (9)	IV	mado		2
kuchi	16	mae		10
kudamono	9	magarimasu [migi e ～]		23
【Kore】 o kudasai.	3	-mai		11
kumori	12	maiasa		4
～ kun	20	maiban		4
kuni	3	mainichi		4
kūrā	17	maishū		17
kurai	16	-man		3
kurasu	12	Marēshia		1
kuremasu	24	massugu		23
kuroi	8	mata		14
kuruma	13	Mata aimashō.		25
kusuri	9	Mata ashita.		6
kutsu	6	Mata kimasu.		14
kyō	4	Mata kondo onegai-shimasu.		22
kyōdai	11	matchi		2
kyoka	17	Matte iru yo.		20
kyonen	5	Matte kudasai.		2
kyōshitsu	3	mawashimasu		23
kyū (9)	IV	me		16

234

megane	22	motte kimasu	22
meishi	24	motto 〔renshū-shi〕 nai to	18
mēkā	22	muika	5
-mētoru	18	muttsu	11
michi	23	muzukashii	8
migi	10		
mijikai	16		
mikan	9		
mikka	5	nagai	16
mimasu	6	naifu	7
mimi	16	naka	10
minasan	1	nakushimasu	17
minna	21	namae	14
miruku	6	nan	2
mise	12	nana (7)	Ⅳ
misemasu	14	nanatsu	11
mittsu	11	Nan demo ii desu.	16
mizu	6	Nan desu ka.	9
mō	7	nan-gatsu	5
mochimasu	15	nani	6
mochiron	9	nanika	13
mō ichido	14	nan-ji	4
moku-yōbi	4	nan-nichi	5
mono	10	Nan ni shimasu ka.	16
moraimasu	7	Nan ni tsukaimasu ka.	23
moshi [～ tara]	25	nanoka	5
Moshi moshi.	6	nan-pun	4
mō sukoshi	14	nan-sai	1
motte ikimasu	22	nan-yōbi	4
motte imasu	15	naoshimasu	18

—N—

235

naoshimasu [machigai o ～]	25	― O ―	
naraimasu	7		
narimasu	19	oboemasu	14
nekutai	6	ocha	6
nemasu	4	O-genki desu ka.	8
nemui	23	Ohayō gozaimasu.	Ⅲ
-nen	11	ōi [hito ga ～]	12
netsu ga arimasu	9	o-ikutsu	1
ni (2)	Ⅳ	oishii	8
-nichi	5	Okaerinasai.	12
nichi-yōbi	4	okane	7
nigiyaka [na]	8	okāsan	7
Nihon	1	okashi	24
Nihon-go	4	ōkii	8
ni-jū yokka	5	okimasu	4
niku	6	okimasu	15
nimotsu	11	okurimasu [nimotsu o ～]	13
-nin	11	okurimasu [hito o ～]	24
ningyō	24	okusan	7
～ ni tsuite	21	Omedetō gozaimasu.	7
niwa	3	omiyage	13
Nodo ga kawakimashita.	13	omoi	16
nomimasu	6	omoimasu	21
nomimono	9	omoshiroi	8
norikaemasu	16	onaji	21
norimasu [densha ni ～]	16	onaka	9
nōto	2	Onaka ga ippai desu.	13
nugimasu	17	Onaka ga sukimashita.	13
		Onegai-shimasu.	2
		onēsan	7

236

ongaku	9	penchi	7
oniisan	7	piano	18
onna no hito	10	pikunikku	25
onna no ko	10	pinpon	6
orimasu [densha o ～]	16	posuto	10
Ōsakajō	24	-pun	4
Osaki ni [shitsurei-shimasu].	22	purezento	7
[Iroiro] osewa ni narimashita.	25		
oshiemasu	7	— R —	
oshiemasu	14		
oshimasu	23	raigetsu	5
osoi	12	rainen	5
otearai	3	raishū	5
oto	17	raitā	2
otoko no hito	10	rajikase	13
otoko no ko	10	rajio	2
otōsan	7	rei	II
otōto	7	rei（0）	IV
ototoi	4	renshū-shimasu	18
Otsukaresama [deshita].	22	repōto	7
otsuri	23	resutoran	10
owarimasu	4	ringo	6
Oyasuminasai.	III	robii	3
oyogimasu	18	robotto	17
		roku（6）	IV
— P —		rōmaji	9
		ryokō	12
pan	6	ryōri	9
pasupōto	10		
pātii	12		

237

—S—

		serotēpu	10
		sētā	22
Sā	19	setsumei-shimasu	24
sabishii	23	shāpu-penshiru	2
-sai	1	shashin	6
sakana	6	shatsu	6
[o-] sake	6	shawā	16
sakkā	9	shi (4)	Ⅳ
sakura	8	Shibaraku desu ne.	8
samui	8	shichi (7)	Ⅳ
san (3)	Ⅳ	[o-] shigoto	15
～ san	1	shiken	8
sanpo-shimasu [kōen o ～]	13	shimasu	6
sashimi	19	shimasu [pinpon o ～]	6
satō	14	【Sore】 ni shimasu.	16
【sen-en】 satsu	23	shimemasu	15
sawarimasu [kikai ni ～]	17	shinbun	2
Sayōnara.	Ⅲ	shingō	23
se ga takai	16	shinkansen	5
seihin	15	shinpai-shimasu	17
sekai	25	shinsetsu [na]	8
sekken	15	shio	14
semai	16	shirabemasu	24
sen	3	shirimasu	15
sengetsu	5	shiroi	8
senmon	1	shita	10
sensei	1	shita no 【imōto】	15
senshū	5	shitsumon	21
[Kenshū] Sentā	3	Shitsurei-shimasu.	19
sentaku-shimasu	19	shitte imasu	15

shizuka [na]	8	suki [na]	9
shōkai-shimasu	24	sukii	18
shokudō	3	sukiyaki	19
shokuji-shimasu	16	sukoshi	9
shujin	7	sukunai [hito ga ～]	12
-shūkan	11	[Dōmo] sumimasen.	14
shukudai	8	[Chotto] sumimasen.	3
shumi	18	Sumimasen ga,	9
shūri-shimasu	7	sumimasu	15
sō	2	sunde imasu [Tōkyō ni ～]	15
sochira	3	sūpā	5
Sō desu ka.	4	supana	7
Sō desu ne.	8	supōtsu	9
Sō desu ne.	13	supūn	7
sōji-shimasu	19	sushi	19
soko	3	sutereo	13
sono ～	2	suwarimasu [isu ni ～]	15
sore	2	suzushii	12
sorekara	6		
sorekara	11		
Sorosoro [shitsurei-shimasu].	19		
Sō shimashō.	13		
soshite	8	tabako	2
sotchi	20	tabemasu	6
soto	10	tabemono	8
sugoi	17	tabun	21
sugu	14	tachimasu	15
suimasu [tabako o ～]	6	Tadaima.	12
suitchi	17	Tai	1
sui-yōbi	4	taihen	8
		Taihen desu ne.	4

— T —

239

taipu	14	tomemasu	17
taisetsu [na]	17	tomodachi	5
taishikan	10	tonari	10
takai	8	torimasu	14
takusan	9	torimasu [shashin o ~]	6
takushii	5	toriniku	9
tamago	6	totemo	12
tanjōbi	5	tsuitachi	5
tanoshii	12	tsukai-kata	14
taoru	15	tsukaimasu	15
te	16	Tsukaremashita.	12
tegami	2	tsukemasu	15
tenisu	9	tsukue	2
tenki	12	tsukurimasu	15
tenpura	19	tsumetai	8
tēpu	6	tsurete ikimasu	24
tēpu-rekōdā	2	tsurete kimasu	24
terebi	2	tsuzukemasu	25
tetsudaimasu	14		
tō	11		

240

~ to ~	6		

— U —

tōi	12	uchi	3
toire	3	ue	10
tōka	5	ue no 【imōto】	15
tokei	2	ugokimasu [kikai ga ~]	23
tokidoki	13	uketsuke	3
tokoro	8	un	20
Tōkyō-tawā	24	Ūn···	14
tomarimasu [hoteru ni ~]	19	unten-shimasu	18
tomarimasu [kikai ga ~]	23	ureshii	23

uriba	3	yasashii	8
urimasu	15	yasui	8
ushiro	10	yasumi	12
uta	9	yasumimasu	4
utaimasu	18	yasumimasu [kaisha o 〜]	9
uun	20	yattsu	11
		yobimasu	14

— W —

		yoi	8
		yōka	5
Wā	7	yokka	5
wakai	12	yoku	9
Wakarimashita.	6	yoku	23
wakarimasu	9	yomi-kata	14
wāpuro	14	yomimasu	6
warui	8	yon (4)	Ⅳ
wasuremasu	17	yoru	4
watarimasu [michi o 〜]	23	yottsu	11
watashi	1	yūbinkyoku	10
watashi-tachi	1	yuki	12
		yukkuri	14

— Y —

		yūmei [na]	8

— Z —

〜 ya	5		
〜 ya 〜	10	Zannen desu.	17
Yā	19	zasshi	2
yaku ni tachimasu	21	zehi	19
yakusoku	22	zenbu de	11
yama	8	zenzen	9
yamemasu [benkyō o 〜]	25	zero (0)	Ⅳ
yasai	6	zutto	12

241

新 日 本 語 の 基 礎 I
〈本冊　ローマ字版〉

1990年10月20日　初版第 2 刷発行

編　集　財団法人　海外技術者研修協会
発　行　株式会社　スリーエーネットワーク

〒101 東京都千代田区猿楽町2丁目6番3号(松栄ビル)
電話　03(292)5751(代表)

印　刷　倉敷印刷株式会社

不許複製　　　　ISBN4-906224-50-4　C0081